MW00623448

# Praise for *Radiant Rebellion*

"Karen Walrond is unrelenting and unapologetic when it comes to finding the joy and light in our messy and tough lives. When I found out that she was taking on aging, my first thought was, 'Let's go!' This book is what we need to fuel a rebellion of connection, love, and joy. I'm here for every page and all the hell-raising!"

—**Brené Brown, PhD**, *New York Times* #1–bestselling author of *Atlas of the Heart*

"Karen Walrond has done the work. She has dragged her feelings about aging into the light of day. She has figured out where the fear and self-loathing come from and learned how to put them in their place. She has drawn on much research and her own rich lived experience to craft a healthier and happier way to move through the second half of life. And she has crafted an artful, joyful, thoughtful road map for anyone else who'd like to age expansively."

—**Ashton Applewhite**, author of *This Chair Rocks: A Manifesto Against Ageism*

"Karen Walrond's writing is full of warmth, wit, wisdom, and heart. As I lean into what I hope will be the second half of my life, I am deeply interested in shifting my own perspectives on aging, and *Radiant Rebellion* provides the stories, tools, and prompts that will not only remain with me but guide me as I learn to accept and celebrate growing older."

—**Justina Blakeney**, designer, *New York Times*-bestselling author, and founder of Jungalow

"The gentle, clear-headed way Karen Walrond writes and shares is a gift. I'm as susceptible to anti-aging propaganda as anyone, but by the end of the book I'd experienced a major shift in thinking and held a really positive, bright perspective on my future. I'm forty-eight years old, and this book gave me a calm assurance that the best is yet to come."

—**Gabrielle Blair**, *New York Times*-bestselling
author of *Ejaculate Responsibly*

"Karen Walrond has created what we have desperately needed for so long: a North Star guiding us forward as the years go on, encouraging us to not only embrace but embody the possibilities held within every chapter of our story. In a world where we're constantly looking back and asking questions like 'What do I wish I'd known when I was younger?' *Radiant Rebellion* dares us to look forward and ask, 'What do I want my *older self* to not only know but *be*?' As someone currently in her thirties, I could not be more grateful that I now have Karen's wisdom in my head and heart to help me imagine all the ways my life can unfold and how I might be able to glow even brighter as the years go on. I am not using hyperbole when I say that I believe this is one of the most important books I—and anyone of any age—will ever read."

—**Katie Horwitch**, author of *Want Your Self* and
founder of WANT: Women Against Negative Talk

"Thinking of friends and family who weren't given the gift of old age or even middle age, I'm reminded of the immense blessing that lies in the simple fact that I'm still here. *Radiant Rebellion* is a rallying cry and an invitation to reclaim control over not just the narrative but the experience and the yielding grace of growing older, no matter what it brings our way."

—**Jonathan Fields**, bestselling author of *Sparked*
and host of Good Life Project® podcast

# Radiant Rebellion

# RADIANT REBELLION

## RECLAIM AGING, PRACTICE JOY, AND RAISE A LITTLE HELL

### KAREN WALROND

BROADLEAF BOOKS
Minneapolis

RADIANT REBELLION
Reclaim Aging, Practice Joy, and Raise a Little Hell

Copyright © 2023 by Karen Walrond. Published by
Broadleaf Books, an imprint of 1517 Media. All rights
reserved. Except for brief quotations in critical articles
or reviews, no part of this book may be reproduced
in any manner without prior written permission from
the publisher. Email copyright@1517.media or write to
Permissions, Broadleaf Books, PO Box 1209, Minneapolis,
MN 55440-1209.

Library of Congress Control Number 2023934428 (print)

Cover design: Gabe Nansen

Print ISBN: 978-1-5064-8763-2
eBook ISBN: 978-1-5064-8764-9

Printed in China.

*To Kermitt & Yvette,*
*who modeled for me, my whole life,*
*how to age with adventure.*
*And to all who grow older:*
*May you live curious. Love yourself.*
*And raise a little hell.*

# Contents

## Part I: Ignite

## Part II: Disrupt

## Part III: Connect

## Part IV: Envision

# PART I

# Ignite

# ONE

# Call for Revolution

A funny thing happens when you tell people you're writing a book about joyful aging.

First their eyes widen. "Joyful aging . . ." they repeat softly, as something resembling relief washes over their faces. "Oh, I need to read that book." Their heartfelt reactions invariably make me smile. But before I can even formulate a response, their eyes narrow and they add some version of the following:

"I hope you'll tackle chronic disease."

"You'll address how our looks fade, right? What it's like to lose our attractiveness and how people don't notice us anymore? The ways our bodies deteriorate?"

"I can't wait to read it because all I can think about is how I'm running out of time."

So I'll begin with a disclaimer: If you expect these pages to be filled with anecdotes of age-related decline or misery and depression associated with advancing years, then I'm afraid you're going to be woefully disappointed. I'll instead refer you to the thousands of books and articles available everywhere that focus on all the reasons to fear getting older. But be warned: Long-form writing and blog posts with titles like "Ten Reasons Why Getting Old Sucks" will probably make you feel worse. Even ostensibly funny books—like *I Feel Bad About My Neck*, the national bestseller by the late great Nora Ephron—devolve into gallows humor.

"That's another thing about being a certain age that I've noticed," she muses. "I try as much as possible not to look in the mirror. If I pass a mirror, I avert my eyes. If I must look into it, I begin by squinting, so that if anything really bad is looking back at me, I am already halfway to closing my eyes to ward off the sight."

Our first instinct might be to laugh. Our second might be to wonder what the hell it is we're actually laughing *at*.

But maybe you're hungry for something different. Perhaps, contrary to the messaging around us, you notice that many people your age or older are leading active, purposeful, and joyful lives. Maybe, when you consider the challenges that will inevitably arise in your coming years, you're pretty certain you'll figure out a way to weather them; after all, you've overcome obstacles in the past. Perhaps you dare to believe it's possible to view aging as a full-of-potential evolution of who you are today. And maybe you have a sneaking suspicion that the bleak views of aging can't possibly all be true.

If this sounds like you—or if you really, *really* wish it sounded like you—well then, welcome, kindred spirit. Read on.

When it comes to aging, I'm generally an optimist. For my entire adult life, I've always viewed each advancing year as full of potential, a blank slate for creating whatever I imagined, and an opportunity to learn interesting things about the world. Of course, I'm not blind to legitimate issues related to getting older: physical ailments, the inability to live independently in later years, and cognitive decline are no joke. But as dispiriting as all of those might be, I'm just not convinced they represent the totality of the story of aging. In fact, I don't think that many of the concerns people hold about becoming older are as dire as we're led to believe.

Skeptical? Consider the following: In 2016, a study performed on more than 1,500 adults aged twenty-one to one hundred determined that regardless of any change in physical and cognitive abilities, mental health actually *improves* with age. Subjects in their senior years were found to be happier and more content with their lives than those in their twenties and thirties, despite any physical ailments. "Most people think that old age is all doom and gloom: that physical health declines and the brain deteriorates and people are depressed," said one of the researchers, Dr. Dilip V. Jeste. "In reality, that is not the case. It does not apply to everybody, and in our study of aging adults, their improved sense of psychological well-being was linear and substantial. Participants reported that they felt better about themselves and their lives year upon year, decade after decade."

The good news doesn't stop there. According to the 2020 Profile of Older Americans, published by the US Department of Health and Human Services, as of 2019, more than one in seven Americans is an older adult: age sixty-five or older. This number is expected to grow to be about 21.6 percent of the population by 2040. America is clearly aging. But it might surprise you to learn how few of these folks live in retirement homes: a mere *2.2 percent*. For those who are over the age of eighty-five? *Only 8 percent do*. And get this: these numbers are going *down*. It turns out that more and more— in fact, *most*—older adults in the United States are functioning better on their own. And for those who do live in retirement communities, the news is also bright: according to a recent survey, most staff and managers of senior living communities forecast that by 2023 their business model will be based on a wellness lifestyle with options for care, rather than care-based with options for wellness. Described as "the dawn of a new era for senior living," these changes mean expanded programs in fitness and other activities, healthier diets, and more emphasis on prevention of disease and quality of life than cures for illness. (My friend Valerie told me this certainly is her parents' experience: "My mom and dad and their friends are able to do things like volunteer and even travel with their retirement community," she said. "They're living their best lives.")

And those aren't the only encouraging statistics. Data suggests that when it comes to late-life disability, the numbers are also trending downward. The same is true for cognitive impairment: while Alzheimer's disease and dementia are still of concern, their rates have actually been *declining* over the last decade. The physical, sensory, and cognitive capabilities of older adults, particularly women, are improving.

Let me repeat: for many of the traits of decline that we associate with aging, the numbers have been going in the *right* direction. Who knew?

So if the news is so great, what's our problem? Why do we continue to fear aging?

I suspect that our anxiety around aging has multiple causes, but a hefty portion of the responsibility falls squarely in the lap of the anti-aging industry. The industry grew from $3.9 billion in 2016 to $4.9 billion in 2021 in the United States alone. The *global* anti-aging market went from $25 billion to *nearly $37 billion* in the same period. The success of this industry's products, from pharmaceuticals to face creams, hinges on making sure we all—men included—feel bad about getting older.

What's more, the target group for anti-aging products is getting younger and younger, beginning at around age *twenty-five*. And the marketing is working: a 2017 poll of two thousand women across the United States indicated that 20 percent of women under the age of twenty-four regularly use anti-wrinkle products. Jessica DeFino, a beauty journalist for the *New York Times* and the creator of a newsletter that aims to transform the beauty industry, said it best: "Once they sell you on the idea that you need to anti-age, they have a customer for life. You always need another product or syringe or surgery."

And that's just the anti-aging industry. Dr. Becca Levy is a professor of epidemiology and psychology at Yale University and a leading researcher in the fields of social gerontology and the psychology of aging. In her book *Breaking the Age Code*, she shows how ageism shows up during the entirety of our lives: from the villains in the cartoons and fairy tales we enjoy as kids, to the imagery that bombards us on social media as we approach our teenage years, to the cosmetics we're sold as young adults, to the challenge of finding and keeping jobs as we get older, to the dismissiveness we can face from the medical field in our later years. "The main structural motive for ageism is that it is often quite profitable, both financially and as a means of preserving power," Levy writes. "A number of commercial enterprises make a stunning profit from promoting negative age beliefs. These include the antiaging industry, social media, advertising agencies, and companies that are based on creating fear of aging and an image of older persons as inevitably declining. Together these sectors generate over a trillion dollars a year and have been steadily growing, largely without regulation."

*Over a trillion dollars a year.* Being marketed to is one thing. Being shamed into buying products designed to keep me from evolving into the person I will inevitably become is another. The calculated cultivation of insecurities around getting older for the purposes of making money feels deeply manipulative. Besides, how dare the world assume that my future self isn't something I desire?

Moreover, creating a culture uncomfortable with getting older may even be dangerous: there's data that suggests that damaging views about aging might actually shorten our lives, while maintaining a positive outlook might actually *lengthen* them. In 2002, Dr. Levy published the results from her longevity study, where for twenty years she followed hundreds of residents over fifty in a small Ohio town. The results? Participants with positive age beliefs lived an average of 7.5 years longer than those with negative age beliefs. Even more compelling is her discovery that positive beliefs about aging can actually act as a buffer against stress and memory loss while also boosting physical function and recovery from illness or injury. I don't know about you, but I'm far more intrigued by what can help me live *more* joyfully, not less.

Thankfully, I'm not the only one experiencing a visceral resistance to this culture of viewing aging negatively; a rumbling call for change is beginning to crescendo. In 2021 the World Health Organization (WHO) released its Global Report on Ageism. In it, the WHO defines *ageism* as "the stereotypes (how we think), prejudice (how we feel) and discrimination (how we act) toward others or oneself based on age." According to the report, *every second person in the world is believed to hold ageist attitudes*, leading to poorer health, social isolation, and earlier deaths, costing global economies billions of dollars. After detailing all the ways in which ageism negatively impacts our lives around the world, the report concludes by calling for urgent action to fight ageism and better measurement and reporting to expose ageism for what it is—an "insidious scourge on society."

And so in response, the WHO created the Global Campaign to Combat Ageism, a ten-year initiative to tackle individual and social attitudes and behaviors against people on the basis of age. "Ageism harms everyone—old and young," said Michelle Bachelet, the United Nations high commissioner for human rights. "But often, it is so widespread and accepted—in our attitudes and in policies, laws and institutions— that we do not even recognize its detrimental effect on our dignity and rights. We need to fight ageism head-on, as a deep-rooted human rights violation." Her colleague Maria-Francesca Spatolisano, an assistant secretary-general in the WHO's Department of Economic and Social Affairs, concurs. "Together, we can prevent this," she said. "Join the movement and combat ageism."

When a WHO report names something a "scourge," a high commissioner calls it a human rights violation, and an assistant secretary-general implores us to join the movement—well, you know it's serious.

The way I figure it, it's time for a revolution.

I've always been drawn to antibigotry activism, so the WHO call to fight ageism piqued my interest. Because of my own advocacy work, I hold no illusions about the success rate of fighting any sort of discrimination: biases like ageism, which are so insidious that they affect us from our earliest years, are formidable. Yet despite how daunting taking on such injustice might be, I'm convinced that it's worth it. Even more, I believe standing up for what's right can be a source of joy. In fact, I wrote the book on it.

In *The Lightmaker's Manifesto: How to Work for Change without Losing Your Joy*, I interviewed activists who were fighting for the causes that were most important to them and who still managed to remain joyful— no easy feat, given that, at the time, a pandemic was overtaking the planet, international climate catastrophes swept the news, and national headlines repeatedly shared stories of hate crimes and shocking police brutality, notably resulting in the deaths of Ahmaud Arbery, Breonna Taylor, and George Floyd, among others. Taking the wisdom of these activists and using my lawyer skills honed from years of evaluating evidence to uncover a deeper truth, I broadened the definition of what it means to be an *activist*. Rather than solely describing a person who engages in civil unrest or risks arrest or bodily harm, I maintain that an activist is any person who is led by their values to purposeful action in the hopes of making the world brighter for others. My book further describes how *joy* is more profound than *happiness*: while both words describe pleasurable feelings, joy is more deeply rooted in meaning and purpose. And with those clarifications, the nexus between joy and activism becomes clear.

With their generous insights and rebellious spirits, the activists I interviewed for *The Lightmaker's Manifesto* share how the advocacy that brings meaning and purpose to their lives requires getting deeply curious. Further, they're intentional about learning from more experienced changemakers, and they stay rooted in their integrity as they do their work. And crucially, they practice gratitude, celebrate small wins, practice self-care and self-compassion, and they find ways to play, all of which ultimately keeps them connected to joy.

So when I read the Global Report on Ageism and the WHO's call to action to fight this human rights violation, I couldn't help but wonder: Would it be possible to fight ageism using the lessons that I'd learned from the luminaries in *The Lightmaker's Manifesto*? Could I research this form of discrimination, learn from experts, and practice some self-care and self-compassion along the way?

There was really only one way to find out.

As I write these words, I'm fifty-five years old. When I approached my most recent birthday, in the spirit of the lightmakers I interviewed, I got wildly curious. But instead of entering a midlife crisis—some sort of breakdown necessitating the purchase of a shiny sports car or taking a younger lover—I wanted to know: What would it take to greet this new milestone time of my life in a way that set me up for aging gratefully, soulfully, purposefully? I decided to research all the areas of my life: mind, body, spirit. I was beginning to understand all the ways ageism was surrounding me, but I also suspected that I needed to address some internalized ageism as well. By the end this deep dive into my life and how systemic forces affected me, my goal was to have a clear understanding of my place in the fight against ageism, as well as an optimistic vision of what I wanted to create for all the years that lie ahead.

To clarify, I had no interest in becoming some sort of super-ager, suddenly climbing mountains and running marathons. I've never wanted to do those sorts of things before, and I'm certainly not going to start now. (While President George H. W. Bush might have considered jumping out of an airplane a perfectly sane and appropriate way to celebrate his seventy-fifth, eightieth, eighty-fifth, and ninetieth birthdays, *I am not President Bush* is what I'm saying.) I just wanted to wade through all the "anti-aging" advice out there and understand what it would really mean to live my most healthful, grounded, forward-looking life. I was curious about what it might mean to "age against the machine," as my friend Ashton Applewhite, an anti-ageism activist, would say. "The sooner growing older is stripped of its reflexive dread," she explains, "the better equipped we are to benefit from the countless ways in which it can enrich us." I wanted to investigate the best way to approach getting older, to determine how doing so could ultimately add purpose to my efforts to join the movement to fight ageism.

The result of my exploration is this book, filled with both the wisdom of experts about what it means to greet your future with a sense of adventure, as well as a few experiments that can help with embodying that wisdom. This book *won't* teach you how to "age gracefully" or "age successfully"; only you can define what that looks like. What this book *will* do is share the details of my own self-interrogation and learnings about what it takes to evolve while defying ageist expectations. And at the end of this book, in the Radiant Rebellion Toolkit, I also offer questions for your consideration, so you can explore what it might look like to live your life forward on your own terms. These journaling prompts will help you launch your own self-interrogation into what it will mean to approach your own radiant years to come. And for the record: these introspective exercises work no matter what age you are, whether you're in your twenties or your eighties.

The word *rebellion*, according to the dictionary, means "the act or process of resisting convention, or normal and acceptable ways of being." And so, in true rebellious spirit, I've divided my findings into four areas: **ignite**, where we learn about the origins of ageism, develop some clarity on what internalized ageism can look like, and kindle our rebel spirit; **disrupt**, where we commit "civil disobedience" by rejecting the social norms around ageism and start to redefine what it means to age freely; **connect**, where we cultivate community with those who inspire that new freedom within us (and hopefully, in turn, inspire them to approach their own aging with optimism); and finally **envision**, where we imagine and then create the future we want to see by living our redefined aging philosophy out loud.

When each of us gets curious about what it takes to shift our perspective on aging, and when we envision our future years as a time of coming evolution instead of impending decline, we become like candles. The thirteenth-century Persian poet Rumi said it beautifully: "The candles are many, but the light is one." Each of us lights the way to move into the next stages of our individual lives. And when there's a critical mass of us, we can shift the discourse on what it means to get older. We can collectively illuminate the value that age brings to ourselves, our communities and our world.

Together, we *are* the radiant rebellion. And it's time to raise a little hell.

But first: a story about how it all began.

# Pilot Light

*Good Lord, I've aged.*

I was walking past the mirror in the main bathroom of our new house, which smelled of paint and plaster. We'd moved into our new home only three weeks earlier, and I still wasn't used to the unfamiliar spaces and angles and shiny surfaces. My reflection had startled me. Who *is* that strange woman . . . wait, is that *me*? I barely recognized myself.

I sighed. It was the very end of 2018, and while I was grateful to be in the new house, the feeling was bittersweet. On one hand, my sister-in-law Kate, her husband Nigel, and their three kids had flown in from Cornwall, England, to spend Christmas with us in Houston, Texas. Because of them, the house was now properly broken-in with peals of laughter, lusty singing of Christmas carols, and a prodigious number of desserts, joyfully made by my nieces, Ellie and Keziah, and my daughter, Alexis. ("BAKED GOODS!" Ellie would whoop several times a day, each time pulling the flour, powdered sugar, and mixing bowls from the cupboards. Cookies and cakes were *everywhere*.) The aromas of nutmeg and cinnamon filled every corner, there were bottles of champagne and gallons of rum punch, and I delighted in watching my partner Marcus and his sister reconnect after several years and thousands of miles apart.

'Twas definitely the season to be jolly.

But exactly sixteen months earlier, the scene had been wildly different. Marcus, Alex, and I were standing on that very same land as rain pelted and wind roared around our fifty-year-old, ranch-style, one-story home. Water was coming under our doors and up through the floorboards. About two hundred miles south of us, Hurricane Harvey had made landfall, changed course overnight, and was making a beeline toward Houston.

By the time everything was over, the three of us had waded through chest-deep water to safety. Dank floodwaters had claimed the house and almost everything we'd owned. The year that followed was a whirlwind of finding refuge with kind friends, mucking out our ruined home and razing it to the ground, finding a builder to rebuild, finding the money to pay the builder to rebuild, and finding a temporary place to live while the builder rebuilt. All this while Marcus and I maintained our careers, helped our young daughter navigate her first year of junior high, and slowly replaced things like . . . well, *everything*.

Restoring our home was no easy task. Accepting help doesn't come easily to me, but luckily, loving friends were quick to call me on my ego. I finally came around, savoring the kindness of so many folks who pitched in to help. Every week, Marcus and I would schedule a "rebuilding date night": dinner at a favorite café, where we reviewed our growing spreadsheet to determine what needed to be done in the coming week. With each inevitable setback we were methodical and practical, and we were intentional about celebrating the tasks we'd completed since our previous night out. In the end, we had a lovely house for welcoming our friends and family over the holidays, but the truth is that it was a lovely house we'd never planned on building. We had liked our old, cozy home just fine, thankyouverymuch, and we would have never left it had catastrophe not forced us out.

In short, it had been an emotional, exhausting year. I stared at my face in the mirror, peering a little more closely. I searched for evidence that proved I looked much older than I did a year earlier. I was, after all, fifty-one; it's not like I was expecting a dewy-eyed adolescent to stare back at me. But weirdly, few identifiable signs of aging seemed new. Save for lines when I smiled, the skin around my eyes remained almost wrinkle-free. *Black don't crack*, I thought wryly.

My hair was still dark, thanks to a recent dye job. My skin was sallow but didn't appear particularly elderly. So what *was* it that I was seeing? When I was younger, there was a *sparkle*. Why was it slipping away?

*It's not age*, I suddenly realized. *It's stress.*

In the moment, I didn't wonder at my conflation of stress and age, or my initial instinct that age could be the only rational reason for my tired face. Instead, I felt relief. After all, *stress* I could fix. I grabbed my phone and snapped a quick selfie. If stress could make such a difference on my face in a matter of sixteen months, surely it was possible to *reverse* the signs of stress, right? In fact, what would happen if I made the reduction of stress a priority of my everyday life? Would I, over time, look different?

Since it was the eve of a brand-new year, I decided to make a resolution: every day, I would pay attention to my self-care in at least some small way. I didn't want this to be a "new year, new you" situation: No expensive new gym memberships or restrictive diets. No public proclamations of my intentions. I just wanted to create simple, quick, quiet habits to see what happened. Things like drink more water. Move more. Rest more.

And so, armed with my "before" picture, I began. I bought some prayer beads, and every morning as soon as the alarm went off and before I got out of bed, I would meditate. I did this for no longer than five minutes, repeating a short mantra of intent as I counted the beads, just enough to put myself in a calm headspace for the day ahead. I bought a weighted Hula-Hoop and began hooping to uplifting podcasts and cheery music several times a week. I drank lots of water: I kept a pint glass on my desk, and every time it emptied, I'd refill it. Each night, I would think of one good thing that happened during the day and allow myself a moment of gratitude. And really, that was it. Easy-peasy, most things taking very little time out of my day. And because the tasks were so simple, they became habits.

A year later, I took another self-portrait in the same bathroom mirror, and compared it to the first one. My hair was longer and still black, as I was still dyeing. The lines around my eyes had deepened, but they were only really visible when I smiled. My skin looked better. My eyes looked brighter. Had something shifted?

I would soon find out. In early March 2020, my friend Laura came to town. I've known Laura for over a decade and she is one of my dearest friends. I call Laura the Original Steel Magnolia: a seventh-generation Texan, she is one of those southern-drawled women who puts up with no shit, has champagne on hand should a moment require spontaneous celebration, and will drop absolutely everything to help anyone in need. Despite living a couple of hours' drive away in Austin, she was instrumental in helping our family during Hurricane Harvey: she had mobilized far-flung friends to send us items she knew we needed, from cleaning supplies and power washers to tea for my British husband and guitar picks for our musician daughter. She is, in short, a rock.

So that March, Laura had traveled to New York City and was on her way back home, stopping in Houston for an overnight layover in our guest room. As we chatted, she fixed me in an appraising gaze, and furrowed her brow. "You look really good," she said.

"Thank you!" I responded quickly, ready to get back to our conversation.

"No," she said, cutting me off. "You look *good*. Something has happened. What's happened?"

"Um . . . nothing, really," I said. She waited and stared. I rolled my eyes and then began describing my December reckoning, over a year earlier. We hadn't seen each other during that time, save for images on social media posts.

"I realized that what I was seeing in the mirror wasn't so much that I was aging," I explained, "as—"

"As your pilot light went out," she finished for me, nodding.

My eyes widened. "*Yes*," I breathed. "That's *exactly* it. My pilot light had gone out. And I've been focusing on getting it relit."

"Well, congratulations." She smiled, satisfied. "It's back."

We moved on to other topics, catching up as friends do. The next day, she left, returning to her home in Austin.

And then the following week, the entire world shut down.

The COVID-19 pandemic came as a shock to everyone, and in those early days, our family's lifestyle completely changed. Being in public without a mask felt foolhardy at best; actual socializing was downright death-defying.

It seemed everybody knew somebody who had been hospitalized by the virus. If friends mentioned that a loved one had been moved to a ventilator, Marcus and I would shake our heads in empathy and horror, the ventilator often being the last stop before last rites. Images of makeshift morgues in cities across the globe flooded my news feeds. Marcus and I made a plan and tried to stay calm. "We'll just stay inside for a few weeks," we said, reassuring each other. "Surely it will be over by then."

The virus, of course, continued to rage for years, and by December 2021 my family had taken every vaccine and booster as quickly as the scientific community had developed them. Dying from the virus no longer felt like a distinct probability; still, the rapid mutations left us all wondering how long immunity would last. As variants with jaunty names like Delta and Omicron gripped the world, resulting in overrun hospitals and people suffering for weeks and months with "long COVID," we kept washing our hands and wearing masks. By this point, we had all but given up on nonessential travel or hanging out in communal spaces, avoiding almost every opportunity to leave the house for fun. In some ways, each day felt like the previous one, like we were extras in the movie *Groundhog Day*.

As I read the daily news with ever-present anxiety, I doubled down on my stress management practices. I bought more healthy food, drank more water, and even added some jump-roping to my daily Hula-Hooping. If this virus was going to take me down, by gum, it was going to do so while my pilot light blazed.

But the virus wasn't the only thing to blame for the bizarre disquiet I couldn't shake. As it happened, the coming year I would be turning fifty-five years old. That same year, Marcus and I would celebrate our twentieth anniversary, and our daughter, now eighteen, would graduate from high school and start college. If society was to be believed, these milestones—officially entering my mid-fifties, celebrating two decades of marriage, becoming that somewhat dispiriting term, an "empty nester"—meant that it was time for me to start slowing down. After all, the *Golden Girls* were in their fifties and early sixties when that television show began, and that they were old was part of the gag. "Get ready to begin the latter part of your life," was the world's morose refrain. "Consider all the ways in which you'd like to start calling it a day."

Now remember: Contrary to what my bath-room-mirror-reaction might appear to convey, I'm not one to panic about aging. I'm what one of my friends calls "relentlessly optimistic." Besides, I come from a line of long-livers. My maternal grandfather lived to his mid-eighties, my paternal grandmother to ninety-six. My paternal grandfather lived to ninety-nine and my maternal grandmother to *one hundred and two*. Assuming I don't get hit by a bus (and presuming that medicine will continue to advance in the coming decades), it isn't completely unreasonable to believe that I might have almost my entire life again to live before my time comes. And considering that I've lived a pretty full life to date, worrying about my inevitable death seems like a waste of good, precious time.

But I also know that when it comes to my optimistic outlook on aging, I may very well be in the minority. Scroll through any social media feed, and you'll find you can't swing a dead cat without hitting someone lamenting their twenty-ninth or thirty-ninth birthday, wailing about the passing of their fleeting youth. Finding folks who are at peace with getting older is rare, and aging is viewed with profound negativity.

But for the record, it didn't used to be this way.

Psychiatrist and medical historian Dr. Laura Hirshbein conducts research on the history of psychiatry, health policy, and diagnosis. In her article "Popular Views of Old Age in America, 1900–1950," she describes how society's perception of aging changed over the first fifty years of the twentieth century. According to her research, in the early 1900s older people were viewed as the principal authorities on old age. Older adults themselves were the authors of the most popular magazine articles addressing old age, describing the quality of their own lives or the lives of their peers. Contrast this to most age-related articles in recent years, which are written by medical professionals *about* the lives of older folks.

As a result, society held few real negative opinions associated with being older. "Although there were some who described disability in old age during this time," Dr. Hirshbein writes, "most of the older people who wrote or were interviewed emphasized their strengths as older people and the beauty of old age." She even cites one article from the magazine *Dial*, popular in 1907, that praised "our octogenarians," who "made significant contributions to the nation because of their long personal histories," and declared that the United States had "tremendous resources in the form of older people."

In the decades that followed, however, came two world wars and the dawn of the Great Depression. This prompted the US government to establish a retirement age of sixty-five, attempting to ensure younger workers were able to find jobs. By the middle of the twentieth century, the way folks viewed aging had undergone a significant shift. Older people were suddenly seen as a burden on American society, and more and more popular articles about aging were written by economists and physicians who maintained that they were attempting to alleviate "a national problem." In fact, according to Dr. Hirshbein, by the time 1950 rolled around, "old age was seen as an economic, social and medical problem that demanded management by a variety of professional groups." Even more alarming, Dr. Hirshbein describes how in the 1930s, child psychologists first began to expand their work to include research on old age and in their tests and conclusions, established the attributes of children as an ideal, determining "normal ability" for older adults by comparing them to the abilities of children.

Isn't this something? Over the years, the idea of what it means to get older hasn't been formed by the writings and testimonies of people who are, you know, *actually getting older*. Instead, the concept of aging has been shaped by the opinions of medical professionals with a predisposed positive bias toward children, and the government, whose public policy motivations were firmly based in keeping the economy moving. In other words, these opinions and policies were based on broad-brush descriptions and sweeping generalizations, erasing any nuance or diversity of personal experience.

And the worst part? *We bought it.*

Now obviously, science and medicine have a lot to teach us about getting older. Far be it from me to suggest that we ignore empirical data about the aging body. But when it comes to forming our own individual outlooks on aging, we should ensure we're getting our information about what getting older can look like from a variety of sources—including personal testimonies from the diversity of folks who are actually *doing* the aging. We should make certain that what we're reading in magazines and on the internet includes *many* perspectives, not just the stuff that makes for provocative headlines. And finally, when it comes to our *own* aging, we should trust our personal experience as well the experiences of people who are close to us—our family members, sure, but also our friends. If we do, I suspect we'd likely find that getting older looks very different for each person. Most importantly, we'd learn it's not all gloom and doom. In fact, we might begin to see that getting older can be enriching. Pleasure-full. Dare I say, *expansive.*

And so, with the new insights gleaned from this research, I decided that I would take my pilot-light work to the next level: I would prepare to meet this milestone season of my life with as much promise and hope as I possibly could, creating and curating experiences that matched my suspicion that the coming months of birthdays and anniversaries and even launching my child off to college would herald a time of unexpected freedom. After all, soon enough, it would just be my partner and me. Without the need to be mindful of our child's academic calendar I would have more space, both physically and metaphorically, to fill any way I saw fit. I could create practices—sustainable, life-giving practices, similar to what I had done after scrutinizing my reflection in the mirror four years earlier—that would ensure that I greeted the upcoming year with feelings of optimism and opportunity.

And so, as I always do when I have an idea but no clue how to execute it, I grabbed my notebook.

My notebook is one of my biggest tools. In it, I brainstorm, create mind maps and goal charts, put words to intentions and dreams, and clarify my thoughts. Its writing isn't particularly lofty, nor does it boast proper spelling or grammar. But I find simply writing my ideas in longhand helps me to see them in black and white, allowing me to evaluate them in a more dispassionate way, almost as I would if I were counseling a friend.

I had recently begun reading *Atomic Habits*, a page-turner by James Clear filled with practical ways to create good habits, and the research and psychology behind why they work. As I opened my notebook, I remembered a particularly insightful observation Clear made: "The ultimate form of intrinsic motivation is when a habit becomes part of your identity," he writes. "It's one thing to say I'm the type of person who *wants* this. It's something very different to say I'm the type of person who *is* this." He maintains that by being very clear about the identity you want to exemplify—the person you intend to become—you clarify the habits that will help support that identity. Your habits, he says, are how you *embody* that identity.

I grabbed my pen and asked myself: *Who is the person I want to look back at me in the mirror on my fifty-fifth birthday?* And I began to write, in present tense.

> *She delights in getting older. She is vibrant, led by curiosity in seeking an expansive and ever-expanding life. She knows that aging never stops offering opportunities for growth.*
>
> *She has deeply grounded confidence in her own resilience: a knowledge that despite the challenges of life—natural disasters, pandemics, health scares, whatever—she can weather it, through*

*self-compassion and the acceptance of the care of people around her.*

I thought some more.

*She is healthy,* I wrote. *Not in ultra-marathon-running shape* (because who was I kidding, I hate running), *but fit. She's able to go on hikes and go on adventures and do anything that she physically wants to do without pain, other than the delicious ache of muscles moving.*

*Her skin glows with life.*

*She has a sense of style—not so much an understanding of trends or haute couture, but a way of using her clothing, her hair, and her movement in a way that conveys a love of life and living, and the values that are most important to her.*

*She has a deep knowledge in where she comes from: who she is, who her ancestors were who came before her. She exudes pride in her history.*

*She has a spiritual practice that connects her inner divinity to a higher power. She continues to express gratitude for little things and makes a habit of celebration.*

*She does purposeful and meaningful work and imbues her life with creativity. She is deeply connected and cultivates community.*

*She embraces adventure again. She tries new things and visits new places. She explores.*

I looked back at what I'd written and felt over-come with emotion. This felt right; this is *exactly* who I wanted to be. Now, having clarified what I was hoping to cultivate in my life, all I needed to do was to come up with practices that could help me make it happen. I wasn't entirely sure what the habits the woman I'd described in my notebook would have. But I knew, just as I did in restarting my pilot light, that having a mind-set of experimentation and curiosity would likely get me there.

And thankfully, there was no reason to go it alone. Luckily, I have friends who are experts, who live lives that each resemble, in part, what I was hoping to create for myself, and whose wisdom would be invaluable. Folks like Tarana Burke, the activist and humanitarian who launched the #MeToo movement, and who takes the lessons from her personal evolution as she grows older to frame her culture-shifting work on behalf of survi-vors of sexual violence. People like Dr. Reeta Achari, a trailblazer focused on the ways nutrition impacts neu-rology and the founder of the Nutritional Neurology Institute. And Brené Brown, pioneering researcher on shame, empathy, and connection, who could share with me her work and wisdom on how belonging can help enhance well-being.

(Incidentally, a note about these experts: One of the insidious ways that ageism shows up is when we attach meanings to the number of years we've been alive, based on stereotypes we hold about those ages. For this rea-son, while I've been quite open about my own age, as you meet each of these amazing folks and to the extent that they don't divulge their ages themselves, I've with-held any information about how old they are. I think it's important that you take in their advice without a lens clouded by any connotations that might arise by knowing their ages. Suffice to say that the people to whom I turned for their expertise range in age from their mid-forties to their mid-eighties, and each of those four decades is represented.)

I knew this experiment wasn't going to be easy and would take considerable commitment on my part. But I was eager to explore how to approach my mental, emotional, and even spiritual health, not to mention what it would take to design new, creative tasks and experiences I could introduce to this new, expanding life. By interviewing these friends, implementing small practices they recommended in my daily life, and capturing what resulted in my notebook, perhaps I could evolve closer to the person who I'd described in its pages. And maybe, in the process, I could redefine what it means to age, in a way that defies social norms and expectations.

I was optimistic. Energized, even.

But first up: quelling the nagging feeling that I had some of my own internalized ageism I needed to address.

# PART II

# Disrupt

# THREE

# Age of Rebellion

*M*an, *I should know better than doing this kind of work in my forties.*

It was 2012 and I was in East Africa, hired by an advocacy group as a photojournalist to capture images of advancements in the fight against extreme poverty. On this day, we were visiting a subsistence farmer in the Great Rift Valley who had made impressive strides in both food security and health care for his family. The farmer's land was located about a mile from our meeting point, down a dusty path through high grasses. With the sun high in the sky, our guides told us the trek would take about fifteen minutes.

Our group was moving at a fast clip, and although the day wasn't particularly warm, I worked up a sweat. Most of my gear, except for a camera with a large lens slung around my neck, was in a backpack. As we hiked, I was startled by how easily I lost my breath. *When I was young, I would scamper over rocky trails like these with absolutely no problem,* I thought to myself. *I should've done this twenty years ago, not now.*

Let's stop for a second and examine how ridiculous this self-talk was. There I was in a foreign land, carrying at least twenty-five pounds of camera equipment over unfamiliar terrain, and my immediate assumption was that any challenge I was experiencing had to be due to my age. As I navigated those dusty Kenyan trails, it never entered my mind that the scampering ease of my youth might be rooted in the fact that back then I scampered every day. Besides, despite knowing ahead of time that this trip to Africa might require some hiking, I hadn't prepared by exercising or increasing the movement of my relatively sedentary body in the weeks leading up to the trip. I could've at least carried my photography gear with me on my short daily walks on the manicured trails near my house, just to get used to the extra weight.

Assuming *age* was to blame, rather than simply lack of fitness: it was just faulty reasoning. Had I simply put in a bit of work beforehand, scrambling over uneven terrain in the Great Rift Valley would likely have come more easily. Ageist thinking is insidious, and even more stunning is how easy it is to internalize it against *ourselves*.

Soon after my trip to Kenya, I learned that this type of thinking wasn't just for forty-somethings. I was having dinner with a friend who had recently celebrated her twenty-ninth birthday. She wasn't very happy about it. Her thirtieth birthday felt like a deadline, a looming reminder of everything she had yet to accomplish. "I can't help but think that I'm running out of time," she moaned.

I suppressed an eyeroll. Good Lord. At thirty, I was only just beginning to feel like a grown-up. "Oh, honey," I said in my most world-weary voice, "the truth is you've only just *begun*. You've finally approached adulthood— and *you've got so many more adulthoods ahead of you*."

Looking back at that conversation, I'm a bit embarrassed. While well-meaning, my response was tinged with pity and condescension. It was also hypocritical, to say the least, given my thoughts about myself just a few weeks earlier on that dusty Kenyan trail. Clearly, I'm no enlightened Buddha when it comes to ageism. As wise as I'd presumed myself to be back then, a decade later my impatience with my younger friend seems almost . . . well, childish. Besides, I'm learning that our opinions on our own aging seem to shift and morph as we get older. This certainly seemed to be the case for novelist Penelope Lively.

Lively wrote her memoir *Dancing Fish and Ammonites* when she was eighty years old. Its 234 pages include her considered thoughts on aging. It's a delicious book, and this particular passage, which appears near the beginning, turned me inside out:

> Years ago, I heard Anthony Burgess speak at the Edinburgh Book Festival. He was impressive in that he spoke for an hour without a single note, fluent and coherent. But of the content of his talk, all I remember are his opening words: "For me, death is already sounding its high C." This was around 1980, I think, so he was in his early sixties at the time, and died in 1993. I was in my late forties, and he seemed to me—not old, exactly, but getting on a bit. Today, people in their sixties seem—not young, just nicely mature. Old age is in the eye of the beholder. I am eighty, so I am old, no question.

And then later, describing her life in the '90s, she writes: "We are into the 1990s here, and I have hit sixty. I don't remember feeling especially bothered about this—full of energy still, writing, living. The view from eighty says: huh! a mere slip of a girl—just you wait." I love that her view from eighty considers herself at sixty to be "a mere slip of a girl." I love that she considers sixty to be simply "nicely mature." Age, it seems, ain't nothin' but perspective.

Even with my emerging awareness about the way in which age perception evolves, I still occasionally fall into some problematic habits. Sometimes I wonder at a minor ache, fearful it's a sign of my impending age-related demise. Or I feel an uncomfortable pang of pride when people say, "My goodness, you look great for your age!" And—guilty admission—I've been known to pause my scrolling if a canny marketer inserts an "anti-aging superfood" recipe in my social media feed.

Is it possible that these reactions indicate some pretty ugly preconceptions that I hold about older people and aging? What if the ageism we see around us is not merely external but internal? And even worse: *What if we're not even aware of it?*

For some answers, I turned to a new friend. Ashton Applewhite is a writer and self-described "pro-aging radical." She makes it her mission to help people fight ageism, both in society and within themselves. Her TED Talk "Let's End Ageism," which has been viewed over one million times, introduced me to the term *internalized ageism*. I immediately purchased her book, *This Chair Rocks: A Manifesto Against Ageism*, and proceeded to have my mind blown.

"Like racism and sexism, ageism is not about how we look," she writes in her introduction. "It's about what people in power want our appearance to mean. As I've gone on this journey from the personal to the political, it's become clear that ageism is woven deeply into our capitalist system, and that upending it will involve social and political upheaval."

Wow. Talk about a call to action! I knew immediately that I needed to speak with her about ageism generally, and how we internalize it specifically. I was thrilled when she agreed to meet with me. We settled in to speak one day via videoconference, and she popped onto my screen from a sunny spot at a friend's house. "I'm so excited to meet you, Ashton," I began. "Your TED Talk was illuminating. And I must tell you, the thing that struck me about it was that it was so . . . *logical*."

"Thank you," she said, grinning widely. "I'm a super logical, nerdy person, but I know that facts don't change people's minds; stories change people's minds. So I have to get better at attaching a story to the fact. But the truth is that the facts alone make so head-smackingly obvious all the ways in which age equity is important."

"Well, your work certainly makes it head-smackingly obvious," I agreed. "What was it that got you initially interested in age equity and anti-ageism work?"

"I wish there was a feel-good or feel-bad story about that—a moment when someone said something cruel like, 'Get out of my way, you old hag!' But honestly, it all began when my mother-in-law mentioned that she was asked all the time: 'When are you going to retire?' And she encouraged me to write a book about this expectation people hold about the right time to retire. So I began interviewing people who were over the age of eighty and still working."

"Okay, that's pretty cool," I smiled.

"It was! But mostly, it was useful for me to meet and speak directly with actual people, because I discovered how different from each other they were, and how they were out in the world in all these interesting ways. And it also became obvious to me very early on that ageism is a huge problem. Within months of doing those background interviews, I had learned all the various facts and statistics that I shared in my TED Talk, twelve years later."

Ashton was referring to the surprising facts I mentioned at the beginning of this book: things like only a small percentage of older Americans ever actually end up in nursing homes, and that dementia rates are dropping in older Americans, not rising. She also shared that widespread and inaccurate impression that the elderly are often depressed: studies show people are happiest both at the beginning *and* at the ends of their lives, simply by function of how aging itself affects the brain. And here's my personal favorite: There's a growing body of research that indicates attitudes toward aging affect our minds and bodies on a cellular level. People with more positive attitudes toward aging actually walk faster, heal quicker, do better on memory tests, and live longer.

A slight digression: the points that Ashton makes in her TED Talk are just the tip of the good news iceberg. You probably know we're living longer than our ancestors. In 1900, for example, the average life expectancy was forty-seven; nowadays, if you're fifty, you may well have half your life ahead of you. For this reason, we can impact our worlds in ways that our forebears could never have imagined. Jo Ann Jenkins, the CEO of the AARP and author of the book *Disrupt Aging: A Bold New Path to Living Your Best Life at Every Age*, writes, "We have a 'longevity bonus' of years—most of them spent in relatively good health—to pursue happiness, help others, serve our nation, give of ourselves to a cause or a purpose that we believe in, and lead positive social change that will make our country—and our world—better for all our citizens." How's that for a glimpse of a whole new realm of possibilities ahead of us?

As Ashton and I spoke, I wondered out loud that most folks seem unaware of these facts about aging. Her response was matter-of-fact. "They don't know about them because we live in an ageist, sexist, capitalist patriarchy," she said. "Also, fear is profitable."

I nodded in agreement. "I believe you. It's only recently that it dawned on me I'm *supposed* to feel bad about getting older, just so that somebody can make money off my despair."

"Yes! There are huge structural forces at work here. And the task for people like you and me is to encourage individuals to zoom out and see them, not focus on our personal 'failings' that 'need to be fixed.'"

"Well," I admitted, "I'd love to think that I'm enlightened enough to do that, but frankly, I'm not so sure. I *thought* I was. Before I'd seen your talk and read your book, I assumed I couldn't be ageist, because of my previous role as an in-house attorney. After all, it had been my job to look out for age discrimination. But then your words made me realize that I *do* make broad generalizations about people on the basis of their age or compare how I look to folks who tell me they're the same age as I am. Honestly, it might be a problem."

"Well," she grinned. "I hate to tell you this, but you do know that in the course of writing your book, you're not going to leave your old life of ageism and age bias behind and start a new enlightened life, right?"

Of course, she was right. We're so steeped in ageism from a shockingly young age that there's no way I would be able to rid myself of it as easily as I hoped. As Ashton writes in her book, research indicates children begin to formulate negative stereotypes about old age in early childhood—interestingly, around the same time they're developing their perceptions about race and gender. I can certainly remember times when, as a child, I felt frightened when meeting unfamiliar older people. I'm not sure I can articulate why, but it might have something to do with the way that the older people in so many of the fairy tales I loved—the stepmother in *Cinderella*, Ebenezer Scrooge in *A Christmas Carol*, the queen in *Snow White*—were portrayed as unsympathetic, or evil, or just plain scary. One of the most popular stories in Trinidadian folklore, told to many a young child, is about the *soucouyant*. By day she's a stooped and reclusive old woman, ignored by most. But at night, the *soucouyant* sheds her skin and travels as a vampiric ball of fire, sucking the blood of her victims while they sleep in their beds. Terrifying! Given that older characters in children's stories are painted in such a harsh and ominous light, is it any wonder that we grow up believing that old age is something to be feared?

"You've had tons of conversations with folks, many of whom have tackled their own ageism with varying degrees of success," I said to Ashton now. "What are the most common messages of internalized ageism that people can't help but cling to?"

"Well, the overarching one, of course," she began, "is that aging is negative. That aging is a bad thing." I squirmed with recognition. "I think it's a super-important point to remember that *aging is living*. We're aging from the minute we're born. So it's inaccurate to say something about the 'aging part of life,' because there *is* no 'aging part of life.' Aging is living, living is aging."

Another message of internalized ageism, she told me, is the thinking that older people are all basically the same. "The truth is that the longer we live, the more different from one another we become," Ashton said. "I mean, all stereotypes are stupid and wrong, but it's particularly absurd and illogical to generalize about older people, because we age at different rates—

developmentally, physically, cognitively. So twenty-seven-year-olds have a lot more in common—developmentally, physically, cognitively—than fifty-seven-year-olds, who are way more alike than eighty-seven-year-olds."

*Aging is living, living is aging.* Ashton's words sounded so obvious, but also so revolutionary. I wondered if that simple phrase might help me tackle my own internalized ageism. But I also wondered if ageism showed up differently depending on where you are in the world, or the culture in which you are raised. Surely there must be countries in the world where people aren't bombarded by advertisements for anti-aging creams and plastic surgery? Surely there were places in the world where aging is viewed positively?

That day I was struggling with my camera equipment in Africa, I met Mike Gebremedhin, a development outreach and communication officer with USAID. "Nice camera," he had said when he approached me, carrying his own camera with an impressive lens. Mike and his colleagues were joining us for that day's visit, and I learned that despite his American accent picked up while attending university in the United States, he had grown up in Kenya. I liked him immediately.

We bonded over lenses and f-stops before we were both invited to join our guides and begin making our way down that narrow, uneven path to the farmer's homestead. As we went, I fell in step directly behind Mike when suddenly, to my left, I noticed an elderly woman standing to the side of the path. She was watching our little procession. Her face was weathered, and she stood erect with her arms akimbo; her brow was furrowed as if she were confused, or maybe even a little irritated by all the ruckus in her normally quiet neighborhood. I averted my gaze so that I wouldn't make eye contact.

Ahead of me, Mike did the exact opposite. "Hujambo, Mama," he said in a quiet voice and smiling directly at her, without breaking stride. *Hello, Mama, how are you?*

"Sijambo, Mwanangu," she responded immediately, her scowl still intact, but her tone soft and kind. *I'm fine, my son.*

It happened so quickly, and we kept on our path, but I couldn't help but be moved by this little interaction. I didn't understand the Swahili in the moment, but I was still charmed by the way Mike called her Mama and the way she received his greeting, without hesitation or suspicion. Years later, when I mentioned the memory to Mike, he grinned.

"Well, first of all, I don't remember that interaction, but it sounds very typical. I'm ethnically Eritrean, I was born in Ethiopia and I grew up in Kenya, so I consider myself an East African. I have a bit of all those places in me. And in all those places, without exception, there's a reverence for elders and the previous generation, even if they're complete strangers. I think it's the way we are engineered. So I'm not at all surprised by that interaction you described, and I'm completely chuffed that you remembered it!"

I smiled. "It was a lovely moment! So given the reverence for older people in East Africa, would you say that people view *their own* aging differently there?"

He considered for a moment. "Having lived for several years in the US, I certainly think aging is viewed differently in Africa. I think there's a certain thing about growing old in the US that it becomes all about how much you produce, how much you work, how much you earn, and what it is that you contribute in a substantial way to society. And once you stop doing that, it's in an American's nature to say, 'Well, I'm just contributing zero, now.' And I think it's the reverse in societies in Africa. I mean, in Africa, people go to elders for advice or their thoughts. The older you become, there's a respect, a deference. In the United States, people often fear getting old because they feel like they're not a contributing or working member of society. They're *dependent*, as opposed to having people depend on them, and I think that lowers their value in society's eyes, and that probably reflects on their own self-worth, to a certain extent. In Africa, I don't think that happens."

Dr. Becca Levy, the professor of epidemiology and psychology at Yale University that I mentioned at the beginning of this book, also noticed this difference among cultures. In her book, *Breaking the Age Code: How Your Beliefs About Aging Determine How Long & Well You Live*, she writes, "The Japanese treated old age as something to enjoy, a fact of being alive, rather than something to fear or resent. In the US, it was a different cultural picture. Everywhere I looked, in TV shows, in fairy tales, and online, old age was treated as though it meant forgetfulness, weakness and decline."

So if you're reading these words and you're cringing with self-awareness at the way you may have negatively viewed aging in the past, give yourself some grace: chances are you've had this type of thinking ingrained in you for a long time. And even those who have made the study of ageism their life's work still struggle.

"I still sometimes fall into the knee-jerk reaction that old equals icky or bad, and young equals energetic, sexy, positive, adaptive, or whatever," Ashton Applewhite told me. "But a really good way to become conscious of these ageist reactions is to think about how you use the words 'old' and 'young.'"

"I don't think I understand," I said.

"Well," she began, "for instance, I hear people say all the time, 'I don't feel old.'"

I raised an eyebrow. "Yeah, I say that all the time. I *don't* feel old. Why is that problematic?"

Ashton smiled. "Well," she said, her voice gentle, "I think what you really mean is, 'I don't feel invisible. I don't feel sexless. I don't feel incompetent.' And I don't know about you, but I had spells where I felt invisible, sexless, or incompetent when I was *thirteen*."

She stopped to let it sink in. "Those words aren't age-related."

My eyes widened. "Oh my gosh," I breathed. "you're *right*."

"It's the same with supposedly positive phrases, like 'She acts so young,' or 'She's young at heart.' What does that even mean? There's no real meaning. When people say those things, they usually mean, 'She's so energetic.' Or 'curious.' Or 'willing to take a chance.' And let's face it: a lot of older people are way more willing and able to take chances than teenagers, who are completely and understandably too worried about what their peers will think if they try!"

She smiled. "Age is *liberating*," she said simply. "So we need to be more precise in our language."

Dr. Becca Levy agrees. According to her research, negative age stereotypes or beliefs affect not only our actions and judgments toward other people but also our actions and judgments toward ourselves. "These thoughts—if they are not counteracted—can impact the way we feel and act." Even more importantly, Dr. Levy's research indicates that succumbing to negative stereotypes can affect the way we function: everything from worse memory performance, self-efficacy, hand-writing, and even affecting our will to live. And again, Dr. Levy's research concluded that those with the most positive perceptions of aging were living, on average, seven and a half years longer than those with the most negative views. *Seven and a half years*! If that's not reason enough to begin speaking kindly to ourselves as we grow older, then I don't know what is.

"Here's a thought for you," Ashton said to me, choosing her words slowly, thoughtfully. "Somewhat paradoxically, the world I want is a world where we *acknowledge* age: you say your age, I say my age. In that world, age is out there as a key identifier, along with our race, along with where we're from. But it's also a world in which we don't give as much *weight* to age as we do. Our age says much less about us than we think it does. And honestly, the older we get, the less it says about us. I want a world where your age isn't the top thing on your résumé. It's not the top thing on your dating profile. It's not the first thing we seek to know about each other."

*The older we get, the less our age says about us.* This might be the most difficult concept to internalize, yet it might be the most logical. As we move through life, our individual experiences—how we're educated, the work we do, the places we live—make us more and more different from each other over time.

"You're right," I nodded. "Trying to figure out a person's age is probably one of the first things I do when I meet someone, and I couldn't articulate why it's important if you'd asked me, since really, it doesn't communicate a whole lot about that person. But that's a hard habit to break. How do we break it?"

"Well—and you probably already know this—it is a work of the lifetime to upend the prejudices and stereotypes that we are all imbued with by an ableist, ageist, racist, sexist, patriarchal culture. Our attitudes form in early childhood. So it's really important that you don't think, 'I'm going to be cleansed of this ageism by Friday, and then go out and change the world.' It's more important to question ourselves and our attitudes. Examine our words and language. And get over that first awful hump, which is the realization: 'Oh shit, I *am* ageist.' Because we can't change the world unless we acknowledge it ourselves."

✺

Ashton spoke with me for over an hour and ended our conversation by pointing me to the comprehensive library of resources she shares on her website. Since our conversation, I keep thinking about her words: *This is the work of a lifetime to upend the prejudices and stereotypes that we are all imbued with from early childhood.* I think about her dream of age being treated as simply one of many key identifiers and fully acknowledged, without the weight of judgment that it often carries with it. And I can't stop reflecting on her statement that the words she said are commonly associated with youth— "energetic," "curious," "willing to take a chance"—are often easier to achieve later in life, due to increased self-confidence and self-awareness.

So I made a promise to myself: I would try to actualize Ashton's dream in my own life. I'd try to fully acknowledge my age and my growing older, while also checking myself and my language when it comes to age. Also, I committed to cultivating my curiosity and sense of adventure. After all, so much of living is about remaining curious: about the world, yes, but also about ourselves, and what we might want to continue doing. We can ask ourselves: "What would I be open to trying, just to say I'm the type of person who *tries*?" And then we can figure out how to do it.

I also promised myself that I would seek out more models of people who were aging beautifully and positively. I'm lucky that my octogenarian parents are great examples, whose love of travel has not abated over the decades. (My mother once sent me a text while they were on a cruise. "Look at your father," it said, accompanied by a photo of my eighty-year-old dad about thirty feet above the deck on the ship's climbing wall, as a crew member worriedly looked on.) But it's also important to surround myself with elders other than my parents. As Dr. Levy shares in her book, a participant of an anti-ageism salon she was involved with offered the following wisdom: "To undo the effects of internalized ageism, we have to intentionally expose ourselves to alternative narratives by interacting with older people and experiencing their vitality, their curiosity, their potential." I couldn't agree more, and I hope to strengthen the bonds I have with the men and women in my life who clearly have positive outlooks on aging, and who continue to grow and expand their lives accordingly.

*Aging is living, and living is aging.* Aging is also about adapting: because while it's all well and good to cultivate a mindset that views aging positively, our physical bodes morph and evolve as well. And let's face it, just as the things that my body did as a toddler are different from the things it did in my teens, twenties, and thirties, my body continues to change as I get older, and sometimes in ways I don't see coming.

So if I'm going to adapt, it seems that one of the first things I need to learn is exactly *how* my body is changing, discover what my body needs, and figure out the best ways to treat it with care. That's where my friend Reeta comes in.

# FOUR

# Body Politics

I was on an examination table at my doctor's office, my feet dangling over the side. My clothes were crumpled on the floor, bra and underwear strategically placed under my jeans, as modesty required (but not logic, apparently, given that I was minutes away from a pelvic exam). I shivered in my paper gown as I waited for Anna, the nurse practitioner who had performed my annual well-woman exam for years. Before she came into the room, I needed to gather my thoughts about what I wanted to share with her during this visit.

I'm fanatical about having annual checkups, and I have always been in good health. But recently, I had noticed some changes that I couldn't directly attribute to any specific cause. The weight that used to fall off my body if I so much as skipped a meal now stubbornly clung to my frame. While exercise remained relatively pain-free, I noticed a bit of "crunchiness" in my left knee whenever I did even a gentle jog, which was a far cry from the punishing workout I used to give it at the club every Friday night in my twenties. And don't even get me started on the night sweats: the waves of intense warmth that came crashing out of nowhere, leaving me drenched in sweat-soaked sheets in the early morning hours.

Anna breezed in. "How are we today?" she said, as if we were about to go into an in-depth discussion about her health as well.

I told her about the unusual changes I'd noticed in my body: the stubborn way my body held on to weight, the regular night sweats, the crunchy knee. Anna listened, and then half-smiled. "Well, I wouldn't be too worried about it," she said, turning to her computer screen.

"But I mean, I kind of *am* worried about it," I said. "These night sweats and my inability to lose weight have never happened to me before."

"Well, we checked your thyroid last year and it's fine." She clicked her mouse. "You're in good health. We'll do some bloodwork, but I'm not concerned."

"But what else could it be?" I asked.

"Welcome to getting older, Karen," she said, her eyes never leaving her computer screen. "You're in your late forties. It happens."

She got up from her seat and began her examination. She said nothing to explain whether what I was experiencing was typical or not. We just didn't discuss it any further. As she suspected, everything did seem fine: my blood pressure was great, and my lab work came back normal. And while "you're in your late forties" might be a viable explanation for the night sweats, I remained confused about why my diet and exercise were yielding little to no results.

The entire situation reminded me of a video a friend sent me a couple of years ago, created by the talented women of the Canadian comedy *Baroness von Sketch Show*. The video featured a protagonist experiencing puzzling symptoms and describing them to several close friends, including her mom. "Is it perimenopause?" she asks. "I don't know . . . is it?" each replies. Frustrated, she eventually visits her doctor and tells him what's going on.

"Is it . . . perimenopause?" she sheepishly asks.

"I don't know . . . is it?" he responds.

Finally at the end of her rope, she loses her cool. "Well, *I* don't know—but you're my doctor! Is it too much to ask you to tell me what's going on with my body?!"

"Yes," he says confidently. "It is."

This video went viral, and my friends and I shared it with abandon. "I feel seen," said one. "I'm pretty sure I had this exact conversation with my doctor last week," grimly noted another. The emerging theme was undeniable: few resources and even fewer conversations about what to expect as our bodies aged. I sighed, wondering if it was time to accept the inevitable discomfort I was apparently destined to endure.

After a few years of thinking about it (and further annual check-ups revealing nothing new), the angrier I became. *This isn't okay*, I thought. I mean, of course change happens. But the Baroness von Sketch actors make a solid point: surely our health-care professionals *should* give us information and sound medical advice on how to evolve and adapt with our changing bodies? After all, our bodies have been shape-shifting since we were born. When we're younger, we can reliably depend on our doctors' counsel not just on what to expect, but also how to stay healthy in the process. Why should we suddenly accept you're-getting-older-it-happens-just-deal-with-it as a valid response?

I decided we *shouldn't* accept it and began doing more research.

For the record, here are some of the reasons it's more challenging to lose weight as we get older: As we age, our body composition changes, regardless of weight loss or gain, and fat mass increases while muscle mass decreases. Scientists remain unclear about why this happens. But nevertheless, muscles burn more calories than fat, so our reduced muscle mass means we're not using the calories we're eating as efficiently as when we were younger, even without any change in diet or exercise. This means that folks are naturally leaner in their thirties than they will be in their fifties.

Further, for those of us who experience menopause, there's a double whammy: during menopause, our bodies undergo major hormonal changes, most notably a marked decrease in both estrogen and progesterone production. And wouldn't you know it: not only is their decrease linked to higher cholesterol numbers, but both estrogen and progesterone help regulate appetite, metabolism, and even eating behaviors.

Now before you throw this book across the room in despair, take heart: our bodies actually need *some* fat, because it serves some vital roles in keeping us healthy. First, fat is important for storing energy, which is potentially critical for when we *do* start losing weight in the later stages of our lives, as many of us naturally will. Second, there are a few important vitamins—A, E, D, and K, specifically, important for things like vision, immunity, bone health, and even reduction of cancer risk—that require fat in order to be absorbed into our bodies. Also, fat keeps us warm. It protects our organs from trauma. A little fat is a good thing, is what I'm saying.

Still, the fact that we lose muscle mass is concerning, and not just because we need it to keep our body fat percentage in check. Age-related muscle loss, called sarcopenia, can eventually affect our mobility, balance, and even whole-body metabolism in later years. Thankfully, however, while some muscle loss is inevitable, it can be significantly reduced—and even in some cases, reversed—with lifestyle changes, stress reduction practices, habitual exercise (especially resistance training) and mindful nutrition. And the good news is that it's never too late to begin.

So given the change in the way my body was processing food—even though I hadn't altered my diet or movement in an appreciable way—I decided to give up trying to lose weight. Instead, I would examine my nutrition and my movement practices, to see if my body's stubbornness was trying to tell me something. But this time, I would approach things differently: Instead of being motivated by a number on the scale, I'd just check in with myself and how I felt in my body. And where I could, I'd use other forms of data to determine my wellness. After a year, I'd reassess.

First up, I needed to address my diet. I don't remember exactly when I began understanding that the food I consumed had a direct relationship to the way I looked, but I imagine, like most young women, it was sometime in my early teens. I noticed that if I ate more, I gained weight, and if I ate less, I lost. Back then, losing weight was not that difficult for me; I was, by nature, a pretty skinny kid. But in hindsight, the intoxicating shot of delight I felt when someone remarked on my thinness should have been concerning. When other girls (and quite a few women) would exclaim, "My goodness, you've lost weight!" I felt as if they'd paid me the biggest compliment they could possibly bestow. I took being told I was skinny as a larger compliment than being told I was smart or kind. Like many young women, I would occasionally fall into ill-advised dieting patterns. Sometimes my mother would look at me with worry, and say emphatically in her Trinidadian accent, "But *Karen*! You're too *thin, man!* You can't keep going like this; you must eat *something!*" Only then would I stop trying to starve myself and resume eating healthy meals. Her words were often the only thing that prevented me from dropping directly into the gaping maw of an uncontrolled eating disorder.

Still, as I got older, for years I'd jump on whatever fad diet was popular at the time. There was the Zone Diet. The Atkins Diet. The South Beach Diet. There was the Eat for Your Blood Type Diet, which told me what foods were ostensibly good for my B+ blood and which ones to avoid. I even dabbled in the Cabbage Soup Diet, which provided the recipe for a bland soup that was the only thing you were supposed to eat for two weeks. Given the resulting bad mood and gassiness, I only made it about four days.

So, with this new diet-free approach, what did it mean to try to listen to what my body was telling me? Since my goal was no longer weight loss, I had no clue where to begin. Because I knew very little about nutritional health and what my own body needed, I had no real idea what I should eat to keep my body—*my unique body*—in optimal nutritional shape. I didn't want to consult Google because I didn't want one-size-fits-all answers. My body is different from yours, which is different from your sister's. Our nutritional needs are singular. I have cultural predispositions to the food I enjoy eating: there was simply no way I was giving up a good Trinidadian *pelau*, no matter what any doctor said. The stressors in our lives are unique to our situations, and geographical and climatological restrictions shape which foods we're able to locally access. So how could I learn and discover what my particular body needed and what it didn't?

Then one day, I remembered a friend who I suspected could help. Years earlier, I met Reeta Achari at a dinner party hosted by some mutual acquaintances.

That night, Reeta was acting as sous-chef to the caterer, a well-known restauranteur who had basically begun the local- and organic-food movement in Houston decades earlier. During one of her breaks, Reeta and I struck up a conversation. As we talked, I learned she was just helping her chef-friend for fun and that her day job was working as a neurologist. Even more intriguing, an article in a local magazine had described her as a "brain foodie," with a special interest in the ways our diets can impact our neurological health. With a background in biochemistry, she is board certified by the American Board of Psychiatry and Neurology. But she also brings, according to her website, "cultural philosophies and methodologies from Ayurveda, Chinese and other traditional medicines" into her practice.

It seemed that Reeta might be the perfect person to give me better answers about my health that went beyond the "you're just getting older" message I'd been receiving from my health-care provider. I reached out to Reeta and asked if she could tell me more about her thriving practice, and she gamely agreed.

In preparation for my conversation with Reeta, I came up with a list of questions: How do we know if we're eating the right things? Could my years of yo-yo-dieting be the true culprit of my inability to healthfully control my weight now? Why did working out seem to have no impact on my weight? But my first question was basic: "What, exactly, does a neurologist *do?*"

She laughed. "Well, we neurologists are the Sherlock Holmeses of medicine. We're the people you come to when you've gone to all the other doctors and they can't figure out what's wrong."

"So, you're sort of the doctors of last resort?" I asked.

"I mean, kind of! Traditional neurology is associated with the entire central nervous system and brain. Your nervous system, of course, is in every part of your body, so the practice of neurology can involve the treatment of everything from headaches, dizziness, and numbness all the way to serious things like brain tumors and strokes and Alzheimer's disease. But in my practice, I'm also interested in the nutritional part—the neurological impacts of nutritional deficiencies."

"What kinds of nutritional deficiencies?"

"All vitamins are involved in thousands of actions and reactions in the body every day. And during most normal times we don't even think about them. Let's think about old-timey diseases, like beriberi. Beriberi is a vitamin B1 deficiency, and there is a neurological manifestation of the deficiency. Low B1 causes numbness, tingling, neuropathy, even brain fog; the fun term for it is *encephalopathy*. But it's essentially brain fog, or difficulty thinking."

Brain fog: I'd been hearing a lot that this was one of the symptoms of COVID. "Now here comes the pandemic: everyone is isolated at home, baking sourdough bread, and eating lots of comfort carbs and drinking wine," Reeta said. "But the thing is, alcohol can *cause* vitamin B1 depletion, and B1 is involved in carbohydrate metabolism. Suddenly people begin experiencing brain fog and numbness and tingling. Of course, some panicked: *Do I have COVID? Am I anxious?* They got tested, confirmed they didn't have COVID, and then assumed that it *had* to be anxiety. And so some sought antidepressant and anti-anxiety therapy. But then *that* didn't work; nothing was happening. Eventually some of those people found their way into my office. And very frequently—more

frequently than I would've ever thought possible—
we just give them back vitamin B1, and they start
feeling better."

"This is astounding," I inhaled. "So just to be clear:
You're not saying that all these folks had beriberi, right?"

"No, of course not." Reeta shook her head. "But
what I *am* saying is that many of them had an insuffi-
cient amount of vitamin B1 for their bodies, and their
bodies were signaling this. By simply taking the right
dosage of B1 supplement, we were able to greatly reduce
their symptoms."

I was surprised. I mean, I'd been really good about
having annual check-ups for years, but I was pretty sure
my doctor had never talked to me about my vitamin
intake in anything more than a cursory way. "Why
don't more doctors talk about this?" I asked Reeta. "Is
this a specialty you had to study in med school? Or have
you just always been enlightened about nutrition?"

"Oh, no." Reeta laughed. "I'm a recovering Taco
Bell and Frosted Flakes girl."

I laughed as Reeta began telling me her story.
"When I was in high school, across the street from us
was a Taco Bell, and I ate Taco Bell every day. I mean,
*every day.* And then when I went to college and eventually medical school, I used to eat raspberry Zing-
ers snack cakes and hot chocolate out of the vending
machine. *All the time.* With my schedule, that's just
what I felt I had to do to keep going. By the time I got
to my residency, my meal habits were even worse. All
I ate was Frosted Flakes. Or tacos from Taco Bell. Or
occasionally, for a change, I'd eat McDonald's Happy
Meals. I was on the road all the time, I didn't have time
for myself, and I'd start work at six in the morning
and finish at nine-thirty at night. And after about two
years, I was chronically tired, my hair was falling out,

and I was just wiped out. Of course, I just figured I was stressed and overworked."

"I mean, of course that's what you'd think!" I said.

"To top it all off, I was having terrible joint pain," she continued. "At the end of each day, I would walk in the door, throw heating packs into the microwave, and just lie down with the warmed packs on my knees, because I was in so much agony. By this time, I was responsible for a lot of patients, so I couldn't remain in this state of debilitation! When I went for my next well-woman checkup, I mentioned to my OBGYN that I was having joint pain and my hair was falling out. And she said to me, 'Well, it's probably your thyroid.' But suddenly I blurted out, 'Would you mind checking the vitamin D level on me? I'm reading this data out of Europe that lack of vitamin D can cause joint pain.' And so she did.

"Turns out, my vitamin D level was so low that my doctor was alarmed. She said, 'I'm not even sure how to treat this,' and I just answered, 'Don't worry, I'll take care of it.' When I left her office, I ended up teaching myself how to treat my own vitamin D deficiency, starting with examining my own diet. I hadn't realized how horrific it was. I slowly withdrew from all my bad habits. I began eating more foods grown in my family garden and visiting organic farmers' markets. I began cooking every day, and I started to feel better. *Everything* got better. I was just so overwhelmingly amazed at the power of food—good food, fresh food, restorative food—and how much better I felt. And that was really the beginning."

These revelations prompted Reeta to develop her nutritional neurology program, which empowers her patients to address their nutritional needs in a completely personalized and data-driven way. I couldn't resist. I asked if she'd be willing to take me on as a client. Luckily for me, she agreed.

Intake with Reeta consisted of a full consultation and inquiry into my health and eating habits. "I'm very boring," I warned her, as I took a seat in her office. "I eat well and rarely snack. I drink alcohol, but never to excess. I don't drink sodas at all—mostly just water, tea, and coffee. I don't eat sweets because I don't like them. I don't smoke. I'm not on any medications, and my blood pressure is really good."

"Okay, well, let's take a look." Reeta asked what I ate for each meal, every snack, and confirmed what I drank during the day. After she exhausted all her dietary questions, she fastened a blood pressure cuff around my arm and placed her stethoscope in her ears. As she listened, her eyes grew wide.

"Well, you're not kidding about your numbers," she said, removing the cuff. "These are impressive."

"I told you. I'm boring."

"We'll see," she smiled. "Hop up on the table." And she walked over to a credenza and grabbed, improbably, a tuning fork. While tuning forks are apparently standard tools in neurologists' offices, I couldn't help but wonder what kind of witchcraft I'd gotten myself into.

"I . . . um, what is that for?"

She struck the fork on the heel of her hand and then placed the stem on the top of my right foot. "Feel that vibration?" I nodded. "Tell me when it stops."

I waited about five seconds. "Okay, it's stopped."

She moved the fork to the top of my hand, and I immediately felt a buzzing sensation. "Can you tell it's still going?"

My eyes grew wide. "Yes . . ."

"Okay, let's do it again." She repeated the test a few more times, and every time, the tuning fork was still vibrating when she shifted it to my hand. Then, she asked me to extend my arms and my legs one by one, and she pushed down on them. At one point, I winced.

"Whoa, what was that?" she asked. "Do you have an injury?"

"No, I just have a bit of a crunchy knee," I said. "It's normal."

She raised one eyebrow. "Okay, last test," she said. "Stand up, put your feet together, and close your eyes."

I did as I was told. As I stood there, I swayed a little bit—imperceptibly, I thought, to anyone but myself—but quickly regained my balance.

"Did you feel yourself move?"

"Um . . ."

"Okay, I know you did. Open your eyes."

I opened my eyes to find her smiling at me. "Well, I do suspect you have a vitamin deficiency. Not being able to feel the vibration from the tuning fork and trouble maintaining balance are telltale signs."

My eyes grew wide. "Seriously?! How is this possible? I eat well! I feel fine! What vitamins am I missing?"

"Well, we don't know yet," she responded calmly. "I'll send you to get some lab work done. And then we'll figure it out."

She finished the paperwork I needed to take to the lab, and as I was preparing to leave, she asked, "I notice that you don't eat a lot of dairy. Do you ever eat cheeses? Yogurt?"

"I mean, I *like* cheese and yogurt, but no, not really. Not a lot."

"I want you to start eating yogurt every day."

"Really? Every day? I mean, I'm not a fan of sweets—"

"Eat Greek yogurt. Unflavored. You don't have to eat a lot, but have a single serving every day. The probiotics in yogurt are essential for your gut health. You can add honey if you need to. Or I can give you a savory recipe for using as a dip for vegetables."

"Huh. Okay. Yogurt. Yes please, for the recipe. I'll do it."

I left her office, bought some Greek yogurt on the way home, and made an appointment with the lab for the next day. The lab technician took sixteen vials of blood, like some sort of medical vampire, and then in about two weeks, I returned to Reeta's office.

"Well, your results from the lab were interesting," she began.

"Was it bad?" I winced, afraid of what I might hear.

"No, definitely not bad," she said. "But we can do some tweaking, and there were some insufficiencies that need to be addressed."

She began walking me through the results. Based on my lab work, there were eight (eight!) different vitamin supplements that she wanted me to start taking. And there was more. "Your cholesterol is normal, but your LDL—the bad cholesterol—is high. Also, your sugar levels are on the high side of normal."

She said my levels were "normal," but all I heard was "high." I looked at her, aghast. "I don't understand this!" I said. "I take a multivitamin every day! I don't like sweets! I feel *fine*! How is this possible?"

"Well, we're going to try to fix this," she smiled kindly. "I mean, this is actually good news, Karen. Remember, I usually only find out that a patient has high numbers after they've had a heart attack or a stroke. We can be proactive here, and this is a relatively easy fix.

The vitamins I'll prescribe you are brands and dosages that I trust, and they're all over-the-counter that you can order online or get at any pharmacy. We'll take a look at what you're eating, to make sure you're loading up on fresh fruits and vegetables. Also, if you'd like, I'll go with you to a farmer's market, so you can see the kinds of foods that you can eat to help boost your levels."

I talked with Reeta some more and then left with my list of vitamins. The next day, I stopped taking my daily multivitamin and began taking the eight Reeta suggested my body needed, slowly adding one every other day for two weeks, eating them with meals, and continuing with my daily yogurt.

Reeta and her husband met Marcus and me at the farmer's market the following weekend. As we walked among the stalls choosing vegetables and meat, she informed me which fresh produce would provide me with the best nutrients based on my results, with suggestions on how to prepare them. My reusable shopping bag was soon loaded with old familiar favorites, like cauliflower and leafy chard, but also some items that I would've never thought of buying, like sprouts. "Make sure you pile these on your sandwiches," she ordered, putting multiple containers in my bag. As we walked, we passed a stand of vibrant peppers, prompting Marcus to mention that his doctor suggested he stop eating them, the result of a terrifying episode of atrial fibrillation a few years earlier.

Reeta narrowed her eyes. "I see," she said quietly. A few minutes later, she took me aside and murmured, "I wish, when patients were struggling with a health condition, doctors would determine ways to *expand* their diets, instead of *restrict* them." She continued by describing the kinds of peppers that she suspected would be safe for Marcus to eat.

But honestly, I was only half-listening. *Expand rather than restrict:* this intriguing philosophy seemed important, I thought, as I paid for my sweet potatoes. It felt like a mantra, one that I could keep in mind for more than just what I was putting on my table.

Now, equipped with Reeta's advice and more leafy greens than I could count, I figured it was time for me to examine my movement practices (or "exercise routine," for you fitness-type folks). For context, I don't think it's possible for me to overstate how unathletic I am. It's like those coming-of-age movies where there's a group of children on a playground, and the two most popular and athletic kids are standing in front of a line of their fidgety classmates, taking turns calling out the names of the ones they want for their team. All the less popular kids waiting in line have worried expressions on their faces, mouthing the words *pickmepickmepickme* and not-so-subtly celebrating when their name is called. Soon only one very puny child remains, and the team captain whose unfortunate turn it is begrudgingly says her name while stifling a groan. She shuffles forward, praying that she doesn't make her team lose the game.

I was that kid.

I had no discernible athletic ability whatsoever. I don't say that to berate myself or be self-deprecating: that statement is just *fact*. I had to concentrate when I ran, mostly because I didn't know what to do with my arms. I got winded quickly. I tripped and fell down. *A lot*. Team sports were horrifying events of extreme humiliation, which I avoided at all costs. I faked injuries, headaches, "feminine issues"—whatever it took for coaches or friends who were avid athletes to leave me in peace.

Years later, if I'm honest, I still carry a lot of shame around my athletic ability. But back when I first decided it was time to relight my pilot light, I knew that I had to include movement as part of my work. So I had thought back to my childhood: Were there any activities that involved moving my body that I actually enjoyed doing?

The first thing that came to mind was jumping rope. When I was a child, I had a small plastic jump rope that I loved. I wasn't particularly good at it, but I remember getting lost in thought in the back garden, skipping to my heart's content. And buying a jump rope wasn't cost prohibitive, so it seemed like a no-brainer to try again. I grabbed my journal and wrote it down.

I nixed roller-skating. I wouldn't feel comfortable skating on the street, and I don't live near a rink. But oh, I was *so* good at it back in the day, when every Friday night would find me under the disco ball at the local rink, movin' and groovin' to the Bee Gees and Michael Jackson . . . but I digress.

Then it came to me: *Hula-Hooping.* I never Hula-Hooped when I was a child, but when my daughter was a toddler, I remember taking her to a park where a group of women were hooping. It had looked like enormous fun. Maybe, in the privacy of my home, I could teach myself to hoop? A quick online search revealed that the trick to keeping a hoop aloft was to forego the toy hoops and buy a weighted one. Done. *Click to buy.*

And so, my movement practice had sporadically begun years earlier, prompted by my bathroom mirror moment. Every morning, I would back my car out of my garage and jump rope and Hula-Hoop in its space. I began by doing each movement five days a week for a limited amount of time: long enough to have fun, but short enough that it never felt like a chore. I experimented with listening to different types of music or podcasts or audiobooks while I moved, or sometimes I'd listen to nothing at all.

After a couple of months, I was pretty good at both: I could hoop indefinitely and fluidly jump rope without tripping. But far sooner than I noticed any changes to my body, I was stunned by how much the practice affected my *mood*. It turns out that while I'm not an athlete, I'm wired for cadence: I discovered that the rhythm of both jumping and hooping had an unexpected therapeutic effect. As a result, any time I began my movement practice with my mind consumed by some challenge or conflict, by the end of my thirty- to forty-five-minute session, I found that I was in a clearer frame of mind to tackle it.

As part of my research for this book, I experimented with cadence some more by adding a rowing machine to the mix, alternating with jump-rope days. While over time I gradually added more minutes to my sessions, at no time did I increase their intensity. They were strenuous enough to break a sweat, but not so much that they felt like punishing workouts. "Consistency over intensity" became my mantra.

Over time, I began noticing some physical changes as well: nothing dramatic, but clothes that had felt snug started affording me a bit of room. Because losing weight had not been my goal, I simply took note of the shift but continued to avoid the scale. But there was no denying that I looked and felt better. In short, my pilot light was burning even brighter.

Then one day I was talking to my friend, adventurer Steve Bennett. In his work and travels around the West Indies as cofounder of the website Uncommon Caribbean, Steve has made it his mission to feature "the real Caribbean less traveled." Steve is from St. Croix and, along with his brother Patrick, he shares those aspects of the region seldom featured in travel guides. On their website they focus on everything from the unexpected (like climbing Pico Duarte, the tallest mountain in the West Indies), to the classic (including the intriguing history of the iconic daiquiri cocktail), to the historic (such as Anguilla's sailing traditions). Over a decade old, the Uncommon Caribbean website is filled with breathtaking photography and rich story-telling and shows no signs of stopping. And Steve is in amazing physical shape.

"It's funny," he said. "When I go on press trips with other travel journalists, they're often much younger than I am. And they ask me all the time, 'How do you look like that? I see you drinking all this rum, and partying with us, and you still look like that?' And I'm like, well maybe it's because I work my ass off?" He laughed.

I smiled. "Is that true? Do you work really hard at it?"

He demurred. "Well, kind of! See, my mother passed away at a really a young age. She was thirty-nine, just about to turn forty. I was sixteen at the time, and I remember very vividly understanding that life can end at any moment. So since that time, I've made it my goal to live every single day as fully as I can. And as part of this goal, I created a practice that I call 'thirty minutes for me,' where I spend thirty minutes every day doing little things that matter to my overall happiness and well-being. I find thirty minutes every day to do *something*, whether it's lifting weights or running or even taking a nap. Reading. Meditation. Yoga. I just listen to my body and do what it feels like doing. These days, I'm trying to weave more swimming into my practice.

I try to keep it to *only* thirty minutes, because if it took longer, I'd be less inclined to do it, since my day gets so busy. But I've found that just taking these thirty minutes has allowed me to be more of who I want to be. And keeping this practice feels attainable, even as I get much older."

*Consistency over intensity.*

I told him I had started doing something similar over the past couple of years. "And I've noticed changes, which sort of surprises me, because I had started believing that I would never lose weight or change my shape again," I said. "It turns out those 'lose twenty pounds in two weeks' crash diets and hard-core exercises don't work for me anymore."

He laughed. "Exactly! But I think that so often when we're younger, we do crazy things to try to make people notice us. But now that I'm older, I'm finding that I do this thirty-minutes practice simply because *this is just what I do.* It's not about how I want to *look*; it's how I want to *be.*"

I was encouraged by Steve's words, because they seemed to validate what I was learning about myself: that shifting my perspective to one of *nurturing* my body, rather than *fixing* my body, could profoundly affect how I felt *in* my body. We can put our bodies through punishing exercises and restrictive diets, chasing a particular vision of "anti-aging" that's really code for "attempting to revert to what we looked like two decades earlier"— ultimately, a fool's errand. Or instead, we can care for our bodies in the form of healthy food, and energizing and joy-filled movement, for the knock-on effect that doing so has on our minds and spirits.

They're all interconnected, after all.

After about six months of loading up on vegetables and moving every day in ways that felt like pleasure instead of punishment, I returned to Reeta for more lab work and a follow-up consultation.

"So, Doc, how am I?"

"Well," she began, "your numbers look really good. And when I compare how you looked when you first came into my office to now, I can see a marked change. You look glowy from the inside. You look toned, and in good shape. And hopefully, with the nutritional supplementation and the changes we made in your diet, you feel more energized. How do you *feel*?"

"I feel good!" I thought for a moment. "As you know, when I first started this, I didn't want to do anything that felt restrictive, and I've kept that promise to myself. I added a bigger variety of foods from the market, like you suggested, instead of limiting my diet. And I do feel energized. I haven't stepped on a scale, but I've dropped a few clothing sizes, for sure. Most importantly, my mind is clearer and calmer. I'm feeling, as the French say, *bien dans ma peau*: 'well in my skin.' Which I figure is ultimately what we all deserve to feel."

"Right, exactly," she nodded. "And it's fine if you don't want to get on a scale. Sometimes the scale can feel like a toxic relationship with a mean friend, so I get that. But the fact that you've noticed that clothes are fitting differently is also data. And I can see that you're definitely leaner. This is the direction we want to go: not toward thinness, but toward wellness. And again, you're glowy. You look great!"

We talked about scheduling follow-up lab work in six months and about how often we should continue to meet. After all, there's no reason to believe that my body won't continue to evolve, and that the changes that will arise won't become more complicated. Reeta was encouraging, and I felt relief that, in addition to my annual well-woman checkups, I now had a partner in understanding how my body worked.

But if I'm honest, not every emotion I felt was a positive one. For example, it is alarming that, despite wandering into Reeta's practice and maintaining that I was completely healthy, the truth was that my cholesterol and sugar levels were creeping up. I would have had no idea that they were changing until something went wrong. Given that each body metabolizes vitamins differently, shouldn't it be standard practice that comprehensive blood tests, including complete vitamin panels, be part of annual check-ups? Surely the old adage "an ounce of prevention is worth a pound of cure" applies here! When I said as much to Reeta, she explained how difficult insurance companies make it for doctors to get paid for prophylactic tests. Health-care providers tend to be reimbursed only for those tests that nagging symptoms deem necessary to diagnose a suspected ailment. "The medical industry has turned into the business of disease, and we've forgotten the business of health," she remarked grimly.

It is also infuriating that so little is understood about aging bodies that doctors simply seem to wave away changes that we notice, with little explanation other than "you're getting older." According to Ashton Applewhite, fewer than 1 percent of US medical school graduates choose to go into geriatrics, because "on average, geriatricians earn less than other physician specialties that require fellowship training. This is partly because office visits with olders, who require holistic care, typically run longer than average—a disadvantage in a fee-for-service, volume-based system." In other words, as we get older, the health-care system is already stacked against us. It's no wonder that Anna simply chalked my symptoms up to "you're over forty," without further discussion. From where she sat, there wasn't much more to say. Her valuable time could likely be more efficiently used seeing other (younger) patients with ailments that she understood better and could more quickly dispatch.

And then, of course, there's the issue of access. I mean, how insane is it that the only reason I was able to learn about my cholesterol and sugar levels is because I happen to have good insurance and the means to pay for out-of-pocket fees? What are folks who don't have funds for annual check-ups or the insurance to cover them supposed to do? How about those who can't afford to pay for vitamins? What about people who live in food deserts, who can't easily get to grocery stores or farmer's markets with nutritious food? How are these folks supposed to figure out whether their knee joint pain results from a serious erosion of cartilage or is simply a mandate to eat more fatty fish? I mean, I might be a dreamer, but it seems to me that the ability to adequately take care of your health shouldn't be dependent upon whether you're employed and if your employer offers decent benefits.

So given all of this, how *are* we supposed to take care of ourselves?

Well, let's begin with the fact that we each have the power to cultivate our own longevity. Studies show that only about 20 percent of how long the average person lives is dictated by their genes. The other 80 percent? Lifestyle. Given this, there are three things that we should keep in mind to optimize our health.

First, the medical stuff: if we can, Reeta's advice is that we get regular preventative screenings of, at a minimum, our blood pressure, blood sugar, thyroid function, and cholesterol. "You should have your doctor do these annually," she said. "As you get older, these levels become really important to your overall health. And be sure to ask your doctor about *trends*. Don't just assume that if the levels are fine that you can relax. If they're trending in the wrong direction, then the time to address them is *before* you actually get sick."

I thought of how my own numbers were on the high side of normal, and the ways that I had already begun to nudge them back to where they should be. I nodded.

Second, and this is no surprise: we should make a practice of moving every day. Study after study shows that in addition to buffering against muscle loss, moving every day can drastically reduce cardiovascular disease, lower cholesterol, improve cognition, and even lower anxiety. And here's some more good news: we don't have to resort to punishing, ultra-marathon-like workouts. Researcher Dan Beuttner discovered that in the areas of the world where people live the longest, fullest lives (known as "Blue Zones,"), natural, consistent movement was key to their healthy longevity.

So it seems my friend Steve and I are on the right track. Listening to our bodies and moving them in ways that nurture rather than punish allow us to create practices that are sustainable, and perhaps even more healthful in the long run. When I shared my movement practice with Reeta to get her thoughts, she nodded with approval. "Making a habit of elevating your heart-rate and providing your skeletal muscles some resistance is always a good thing," she said.

"Anything else I should keep in mind when it comes to my health?" I asked.

"Repeat after me," she said. "Eat fresh, eat seasonally, eat locally, eat wisely." According to Reeta, eating locally helps ensure that you're eating seasonally, and by eating seasonal fresh foods every day, even if you supplement your diet with canned or frozen fruits and vegetables, at least you're getting maximum nutrition from the fresh, local produce you're consuming each week. If you don't have access to a farmer's market, consider growing your own produce, since many vegetables can be grown in containers in small spaces. In a pinch, use an app to determine what produce is currently in season in the area where you live: it can help you determine what is likely freshest at your local grocery store. Your local farmer's almanac, found online, can also provide reputable information.

And then she added something that completely shifted how I'll look at food going forward. "So many of us eat solely for diet or for fashion, but we don't eat for nutrition," she explained. "And we've forgotten that vitamins—many of them organic compounds that our bodies do *not* make, and that we *must* get from food—are essential to every single reaction in the cells of our bodies. They're *critical*. So when we look at every day food, we need to look at the nutrition we get from it."

And then she paused before speaking again. "Also, I think the quote attributed to Hippocrates—'let food be thy medicine'—isn't the right way to look at food."

I was surprised. I thought this was *exactly* what she had been telling me. "It isn't? Say more about that," I urged.

"Well, 'medicine' implies 'sickness,' and I think that approaching food from that perspective is wrong," she began. "In traditional Ayurvedic medicine, you don't focus on sickness. Ayurveda is about wellness, and how you nourish the health that exists in all of us. It's how you bring the breath of life into your body. Food is nourishment. Good, whole food is fuel, promoting energy within the body. It's not 'medicine' or about 'superfoods that reverse illness.' Food is about nourishing wellness."

"Oh, wow," I said. "I always considered healthy food as simply food that isn't filled with chemicals or too much sugar or fat: food I could count on not making me ill. Thinking instead of healthy food as a carrier of energy and life to nourish health in my body . . . honestly, that feels life-shifting. It feels revolutionary."

"Exactly!" Reeta was excited now, like a teacher whose student had just caught on to an important concept. "And by the way, this is why we have favorite foods when we celebrate, and we should enjoy them. Food shouldn't be a 'guilty pleasure'; it should be a *pleasure*. Our brains have dedicated a huge amount of real estate to smell and taste, both of which are linked to memory and good health and well-being. Nourishing food should be *enjoyed*."

This shift in perspective, combined with new insight about my own body, has inspired in me a fundamentally new approach to my health. But it mirrors an approach that I've taken in other aspects of my life. In fact, as a leadership and activism coach, it's an approach I often encourage my clients to adopt, rooted in the study of positive psychology.

Dr. Martin Seligman is a psychologist and former president of the American Psychological Association. When he assumed the position in 1998, he decided to make positive psychology—the scientific study of human potential—the theme of his work. As a result, he is now the field's leading authority. Seligman posits that rather than fixating on pathologies and mental illnesses, as traditional psychology has often done, it also makes sense to study the positive attributes and practices that allow us to achieve our potential. In this way, we have a more holistic view of what it takes to thrive. His extensive research has been broadly supported by a number of venerable institutions, including the National Institute of Mental Health, the National Institute of Aging, and the National Science Foundation.

As a leadership coach trained in the basics of positive psychology, I often use its tenets by encouraging clients to take the practices that have brought them success in the past and use them to help achieve their goals for the future. And it seems to me now that what Reeta is suggesting is similar to Seligman's work on positive psychology, except it's about positive *physicality*. She suggests that rather than fixating on our physical illness and ailments, we should equally focus on "the health that exists in all of us," nurturing and developing practices that allow the healthy aspects of our physicality to continue to thrive. She isn't saying that we shouldn't fix what ails us—far from it—but also offers that we should nourish the parts of our body that also *sustain* us. And let's face it: in our day-to-day lives, we can often forget about the parts of our health and our bodies that are actually *working*. Perhaps we should spend an equal amount of time nurturing our health—through nutritious food and pleasurable movement—as we do treating our ailments.

In the end, I believe that taking care of our bodies as we grow older is all about trusting our *curiosity*. We should get curious about eliminating stress by introducing daily practices that reignite our pilot lights. Let curiosity prompt us to ask questions of our primary care providers when we notice our bodies changing. Finally—and this is big—curiosity should keep us from settling for dismissive, incomplete answers from our doctors. Curiosity can prompt us to dig deeper about getting a personalized view of our current state of our nutritional health and the ways that we can enhance it.

Naturally, as we get older, our bodies will change, and it's easy to fall into the habit of thinking that discomfort is just part of the package. But don't accept it without a fight—or at the very least, a little rebellion. Remember, as Ashton puts it: "If your knee hurts, it's not just about how much cartilage has worn away and what can and can't be done about it. It's about what you think that condition says about you, and which interpretations you reject or embrace. If you hear, 'what do you expect at your age?' it's about pointing out that other parts of you are holding out perfectly well—and finding a new doctor." We might need to challenge our doctors to find solutions for easing our discomfort. After all, that's what we pay them for.

Because of this new insight, I'll keep taking vitamins, meditating, moving frequently, drinking my water, and eating nourishing, flavorful foods. My goal is not to develop a preternaturally young-looking body, or even to live to over one hundred, goals that might have been my focus in my twenties. No, my goal is to remain *bien dans ma peau*—to feel "well in my skin." *Curiosity over intensity,* remember. I want to keep my body, mind, and spirit in the best health required to remain curious and optimistic and open, from day to day. Because, really, it is in the living that we create a well-lived life.

# FIVE

# Beauty Myth

"Karen, what is this?"

I was eleven years old and had just begun seventh grade at Kingwood Middle School. My dad had recently received a promotion that required a move to the United States. I'd spent most of my life in Trinidad, and Texas was decidedly different. Back home, my friends and I lived in shorts, hair braided or pulled back to keep the sea breeze from whipping it into our eyes. In Kingwood, the Jordache jeans and Farrah-Fawcett-inspired hair my classmates wore made them seem so much older—and me, in contrast, so much stranger.

Mom was standing at the kitchen table, waiting for an answer. My book bag was lying open in front of her. *Shoot*, I thought. *I forgot to clear my lunch out of my bag.* I searched her face, trying to figure out how much trouble I was in. Her brow was furrowed, but an almost-imperceptible smile played at the corners of her mouth as she held out two small items in the palm of her hand.

I was in trouble, but not too terrible. Best to come clean. "It's makeup," I answered, lowering my eyes. "Blush and lipstick. I bought it with my allowance at the pharmacy on the way home from school."

"Karen, you know you're too young to wear makeup."

"But *everyone* wears makeup at this school, Mummy," I whined. "Everyone in my class is a year older than me, and they wear tons of makeup because that's what's normal here. And they already think I look funny because I'm one of the only Black students in the entire school, and girls keep asking me why I don't wear makeup, and they say that I might be kind of be pretty if I did, and. . . " I ran out of steam. "I just figured I'd try a bit to see if it made a difference."

To my eternal surprise, my mother relented. "Okay, fine," she said. "But no mascara or eyeliner. You are way too young to wear that."

"I promise," I said, and she handed back my lipstick, blush, and book bag.

The next morning as I was getting ready, my mom popped her head into the bathroom. "Have you put on the makeup yet?" she asked, barely able to hide her amusement.

"I was about to."

"Well, there are a couple of things you need to remember," she said, opening the door the whole way and coming right in. "You want to make sure that when you put lipstick on, you go *inside* your lip line. Remember, because we're Black, we have big lips, and you need to minimize their size." She showed me how. "Also, just like blush can be used to show your cheekbones, you need to learn how to apply color to minimize your nose. Black women have broad noses, so you need to use makeup to make your nose appear smaller."

It seemed weird to me that people wouldn't be able to see through my attempts to change the shape of my face, but I nodded solemnly. I carefully lined the inside of my lip line and filled it in with the nude-colored lipstick. I brushed the coral blush along my cheekbones and the length of my nose, a technique I remembered seeing in *Seventeen* magazine that promised to make my nose appear smaller. Then off I went to school.

My friend Lori was the first person who noticed. "You look great!" she beamed, tossing her blonde hair. "I knew you were pretty. For a Black girl, I mean. Now it shows!"

✳

At the time, I didn't know that my mother's advice was steeped in generations of colonialist, Eurocentric ideas of beauty. To be clear, her advice was well-meaning and came from a place of maternal love: it was the late seventies, after all, and we were Black immigrants living in a predominantly white, southern, American neighborhood. Her guidance was intended to protect me from judgments that she knew could be cruel. For years after that morning, I continued to apply lipstick in an attempt to minimize my lip shape and researched new ways of making my nose seem smaller. And during that time, if you had ever asked me about the term "internalized racism," I would have responded with conviction that that wasn't actually a thing. It wasn't until almost two decades later, when a friend complimented me on the shape of my lips, that I considered the possibility that any part of my face that could be remotely considered attractive.

But that's the thing about fickle beauty standards, isn't it? At best, they're shaped by culture and fad, and at worst, by bigoted or racist tropes. Besides, if we've learned anything from Rubenesque images of women's bodies in seventeenth-century art, the waifishly thin, heroin-chic models of the 1990s, and the booty-poppin' curves of today's influencers, it's that what passes for the "ideal beauty" seems to only last for a decade or so. It's a fool's errand to try to morph ourselves and our bodies to keep up, to say nothing of the impossibility of the task when race is added to the mix. As Naomi Wolf famously said in her book *The Beauty Myth*, "ideal beauty is ideal because it does not exist." And lest you think men are immune, in the preface of her updated version of her book, Wolf muses, "As I predicted it would, a male beauty myth has established itself in the last decade, moving from inside the gay male subculture to the newsstands of the nation, and hitting suburban dads with a brand-new anxiety about their previously comfortable midsections. . . . Men are now a third of the market for surgical procedures, and ten percent of the college students suffering from eating disorders are men."

Given all of this, it seems to me that rather than attempting to conform to an arbitrary beauty standard— one devoid of any concept of diversity or variety—we may as well define beauty on our own terms.

And so, soon after that friend's compliment, I began experimenting with what it would feel like if I acted as if the parts of my face that I'd been trying to minimize were, in reality, beautiful. I started wearing lipstick over the entire surface of my lips rather than feebly attempting to make them look smaller. I gave up trying to alter the shape of my nose (since I really had no idea what I was doing anyway). And I even stopped using chemical straighteners on my hair. That was probably the biggest risk of all, since for years I had been told that having straight hair was the only way to be perceived as "professional" in my jobs as an engineer and a lawyer.

In other words, I stopped trying to look like someone I am not. And you know what happened?

Nothing. Nothing happened. Nobody recoiled in horror at my nose or my lips. I didn't get hauled into HR for a conversation about appropriate dress or the proper way to style my hair. (Given that I was in-house counsel at the time, I concede that it would've been foolhardy for anyone to try.) No one seemed to notice the way I changed my makeup, and people even complimented me on my new short, cropped hairdo. I even took to dyeing my naturally black hair color to an even darker, inky blue-black, which I thought emphasized the chocolate brown of my skin. And the world didn't end. The best part is that as I grew more comfortable with how I looked, I became prouder of who I am.

I contentedly moved through life in this manner for many years. Eventually, however, the jet-black color of my hair dye started to feel too harsh for my face. I switched to a deep brown color, but I noticed that between dye jobs that streaks of silver had begun to appear. But by this point, dyeing my hair had become a habit, and at the age of fifty-three, I was coloring every six weeks.

*What am I doing?* I thought to myself one day, my gloved hands covered in mahogany dye. *I'm spending way too much money on this. Besides, putting these chemicals on my hair this often can't be healthy. What if I . . . stopped?*

It turns out that the phenomenon of dyeing hair is a relatively new one. In the early part of the twentieth century, only about 4 to 7 percent of American women colored their hair—that is, until beauty companies figured out that there was a killing to be made by tapping into women's anxiety around aging. And they weren't even subtle how they went about it: one 1943 Clairol ad called gray hair "The Heartless Dictator," stating, "Without justice or kindness, gray hair can rule your life. . . . It can dictate many things you say or do. No wonder other women refuse to tolerate this tyrant." The aggressive marketing worked: Nowadays more than 70 percent of women in America dye their hair. It's practically a national pastime.

The thing is, we often dye our hair without so much as a second thought. In her book *Going Gray*, journalist Anne Kreamer documented her path to silver. As part of her experiment, she gathered fifteen girlfriends ranging in age from their mid-thirties to their mid-sixties to hear their thoughts about going gray. As the women began sharing why they chose to either continue dyeing their hair or stop coloring altogether, it became clear that, until that conversation, they hadn't really examined their reasons for making the decisions about their hair color. "It was as if a lightbulb went off over everyone's head," she writes. "We *sort of* know on a subliminal level that most of us are faking it—these days a majority of American women over forty dye their hair—but we seldom actually let ourselves *think* about this and what it implies."

And so, as I stood there with my hair dripping with dye, staring at myself in the mirror—the same mirror where a couple of years earlier I made the commitment to reverse the stress that had shown up on my face—I considered what coloring my hair implied in my own life. Hadn't I experienced a similar reckoning with the reasons I'd straightened my hair in the past? Were my reasons for dyeing my hair in any way like the reasons I used to justify minimizing my lips or narrowing my nose? Was I coloring my hair because I loved the color I was adding, or was I doing it to hide the color I was becoming? And if it was for hiding: What did that *mean*, exactly?

Ultimately, I decided there was only one way to find out: I finished applying the dye, and while waiting for it to take effect, I made an appointment at my hair salon for two months down the road. On the day of my appointment, I walked in and then walked out with a brand-new haircut: back to the cropped look I sported when I stopped chemically straightening my hair, only about half an inch long, completely dye-free. It was only hair, after all: I'd worn it short several times over the years, and I knew I could grow it back and dye it again if I changed my mind. But for the purposes of my own self-interrogation, I wanted to experience what it felt like to move through life without any attempt to look younger than my age.

If this sounds brave, let me clarify: I was terrified. I had become quite comfortable—some might say prideful—of being told that I looked almost a decade younger than I was. My new cropped haircut was decidedly "salt-and-pepper," and while it was still more pepper than salt, I worried that folks would think I'd "let myself go." What if people now thought that I was a decade *older* than I was? And if they did, how would that affect me?

My mother had an immediate reaction. "You cut your hair! You know I always love you with your hair short."

"Thanks, Mom."

"And . . . wow. Wow. Look how gray you've gotten!"

"Yup. I guess that's what a hurricane and a pandemic will do," I said.

"So you're not dyeing it anymore?" My mother, now in her eighties, had her own gorgeous, silvery-white hair.

"I don't think so."

"Well, you get your gray hair from me." It was true: my father, also in his eighties, only had a smattering of white in his own hair, almost less than I did. "But

I didn't stop dyeing until I was much older than you. Why are you stopping now?"

"I dunno. It's just time, I guess."

She furrowed her brow, and a look of concern spread across her face. "Well, what does Marcus think?"

For the record, my husband and daughter had barely batted an eye. Marcus was already quite silver and had always preferred my hair short, so he loved the cut. Alex, now sixteen, looked at me without any expression: "Oh you've cut your hair again," she had observed, before returning to her phone.

"Honestly, I don't think I care what he thinks, Mom. It's my hair!"

"Well, I suppose that's true," she conceded. "It's a different time . . ." As her voice trailed off, I took the opportunity to change the subject.

While I acclimated to my new look, I began searching for folks my age who allowed their hair to go natural. To my surprise, there were very few. One of them was my client and friend Amy, who has a beautiful mane of snowy white hair.

"I'm so excited for you that you're letting your hair go silver!" she said one day.

"Thanks," I said. "I so love yours. Did you just let your hair naturally go silver over time, or did you used to dye it?"

"Oh, I used to dye it," she said. "But eventually, I was doing it so often, I just gave up."

"Same. Any regrets?"

"None," she grinned. "I love it. I *love* it. I get complimented on it every day. Best decision I ever made."

As time passed, people began noticing my hair growing more and more white. One day, I caught up with Mike, the friend I made in Africa. "Can I just say," he said, "I *love* that your hair is going silver."

"Thank you," I smiled.

"Honestly, I just think gray hair is amazing. I used to beg my wife, Caroline, to stop dyeing her hair, and she finally stopped because it was such a process. It's fantastic! She gets complimented all the time. I love it."

"Well, I really appreciate you saying this. It's an experiment, but it's definitely growing on me."

It's now been just over a year since I've stopped dyeing my hair. I've also begun growing it out again, and at this point it has about as much salt in it as pepper. And like Mike's wife, it's a rare day that I go out in public and a stranger doesn't comment approvingly. On a recent holiday in the Caribbean, the groundskeeper of our hotel shouted to me as I walked past: "Sistah! Ah lovin' de hair, man. Ah does keep tellin' meh own sistah she mus' leh she hair go white-white-white. It does make yuh look like a *queen*!"

While other people's opinions of my hair shouldn't matter, I admit it's encouraging to receive such an overwhelmingly positive reaction. But I have a theory about *why* folks react with such admiration, and I don't think it has that much to do with my hair. I think the real reason that people react so positively is that I'm *comfortable* with having silver hair. In a world where everyone dyes their hair, my silver is something of a novelty. It's almost as if I'd dyed it blue or pink. Because women are expected to hate going gray and fight it every step of the way, folks are intrigued with any woman who is actually okay with the way her hair is shot through with white.

As evidence, I offer journalist Anne Kreamer's words, these about one of the main characters in the blockbuster movie *The Devil Wears Prada*. Kreamer writes: "Meryl Streep played an absolutely ungrandmotherly white-haired magazine editor, the personification of stylish glamour. Almost every review made a point of mentioning her hair color, and in the movie narrative, her public alpha-female self-confidence is reinforced by her tacit refusal to submit to the blend-in-with-the pack camouflage of artificial hair color. According to *Entertainment Weekly*, Streep chose the striking 'Cruella De Vil' look herself, saying, 'In a business that's all about artifice, I like the pride of having naturally beautiful white hair and not coloring it.'"

In a world where you can be penalized for allowing your hair to go silver, the instinct to dye is an inarguably reasonable one. But it's comforting to know that taking the risk to refuse to color your hair can be a form of resistance. And maybe, on the best of days, it can even be sexy.

As I grew more and more comfortable with my changing hair color, I realized that my clothes didn't feel right anymore. Colors that had worked with my black hair didn't seem to work with my new salt-and-pepper hair. Allowing my hair to come into its natural color felt like an evolution: shouldn't the way I dress undergo a similar transformation? I decided to call my friend Stasia to help me think through my wardrobe.

Stasia Savasuk is a style activist and the founder of Style School, a multiweek workshop that helps individuals express who they are through what they wear. Style School has very little to do with fashion and everything to do with what Stasia calls "inside-out congruency"; that is, dressing as a reflection of who we are and how we want to move through the world. "It's taking inventory of who you truly are on the inside," she explained to me, "and determining how can you project that on the outside, so when you look at yourself in the mirror, you go, *'there* I am.'" And Stasia bristles if you call her a "personal stylist." "I don't follow trends, read fashion magazines, adhere to style 'rules,' or place anyone into 'boxes,'" she told me. "I don't do makeovers."

Stasia's work began when her daughter Raisa saw herself in the living room mirror. "For years, I had coerced her into wearing dresses, even though she hated them," Stasia recounted to me. "When she was six years old, she talked me into buying her a shirt and tie at a local thrift shop, and when she got home, she put them on, looked at herself in the mirror and she took her own breath away. It was like she finally recognized herself. And it was such a mind-blowing moment for me, because at that point, I don't think *I* had ever looked in the mirror and taken my own breath away."

I'm a past student of Stasia's Style School. A few years ago, I had realized that everything in my closet was black or dark grey. I wish I could say it was because I loved the elegance of both colors, but it was because I'd read somewhere that black is slimming. The motivation—trying to minimize who I was by wearing black—felt embarrassingly close to the way I'd used makeup when I was a kid to hide the fullness of my lips or broadness of my nose.

I had decided that I wanted to start playing with color in the same way I'd begun using makeup to express, rather than hide. Intrigued by Stasia's philosophy—that we can choose attire not by trends or body shape but by how the clothes make us feel—I enrolled in Style School. Serendipitously, the session was scheduled for the months following Hurricane Harvey, when I'd lost everything in my closet. Given that I needed to replace my clothing anyway, it was the perfect time to examine my relationship with clothes, with Stasia's guidance. I made my way through her program and was surprised to learn that some colors make me feel brighter, more confident, and more alive. Nowadays, it's rare that I wear all black.

Still, it had been a few years since Style School, and so much had changed in the intervening years: my hair color, sure, but also the rebuilding of our life after Harvey. It's pretty impossible to reconstruct a whole new life *and* live through the impact of a global pandemic and come out unscathed on the other side. I wasn't the same person I was when I had taken Style School in the immediate aftermath of the storm. So I reached out to Stasia to ask her how I should approach this new evolution in my clothing, since I was beginning to feel like my current style didn't work for me anymore. "How do I do it?" I asked. "I have all the tools from Style School, but this feels more like a revamp than an overhaul. Should I just go to Pinterest and start pinning looks I like? Start buying magazines? What do I do?"

"Well," she said, "as you know, one of the questions I always ask clients when they try on a new piece of clothing is how it makes them *feel*. And you can't really tell how something will make you *feel* by looking at a photograph. I understand the allure of finding images that inspire us, but I think it's really, really important to interrogate ourselves: Are we attracted to what that person is *wearing*, or are we attracted to their *congruency*? We often don't know the difference. And this can be the downside of Pinterest, because sometimes what we're really responding to in an image is the person's *vitality*, and then we pin their *outfit*. It's their *essence* we're attracted to, and it's reflected in what they're wearing—but it's not actually the *clothes*. The way you'll find your own congruency won't be by wearing exactly what someone else is wearing, because that might not feel congruent for you. It's a nuance-y difference and the discernment takes a lot of practice. Frankly, I'd just start by shopping your closet. By going through each item and examining what feels right, you'll probably discover you already own much of what you need; you just need to wear items in different combinations or in different ways to feel right."

This made a lot of sense, and honestly, it was kind of a relief. "Shopping my closet" sounded a lot less expensive than springing for a whole new wardrobe.

"Is it just me?" I asked Stasia. "Do you find that you're constantly having to evolve as well? Has your approach to practicing and experimenting changed as you've gotten older?"

She thought for a second. "I think it has less to do with aging," she answered slowly, "and more to do with *maturing*."

I asked her to say more. "Well, one of the things that I'm learning as I grow older is that I want to take up space," she said. "For example, my word of the year is *expand*. I want my work and life to be about *expansion* and finding safety in joy and abundance. So because I use these words as inspiration, I find myself attracted to wide silhouettes that embody these concepts. I'm wearing more wide-legged pants and oversized tops, which make me feel expansive and like I'm taking up space, and I'm loving them. Wearing oversized clothing with big lapels is new for me, because I've always worn leggings, little skirts, little jackets. And the reason I'm able to do this is because I've healed from previous self-talk that says, 'Don't take up space.' So it's not so much an age thing as a maturity thing. It's maturing into my body. And I'm practicing how I want to show up, but also doing it in a way that I can look at myself with love."

This was new: when I first participated in Style School, much of what I learned was about checking in with myself *in the moment*, when I put on something to wear for the day. Hearing how Stasia uses the word "expansive" as an overarching concept and guiding principle for how she wants to show up in the world, it felt like getting an advanced-level lesson on how to approach my closet as a whole. Naturally, the idea of "expansiveness" resonated with me. That word kept coming up with everyone to whom I'd been speaking. But I knew I'd already come up with my own language and words at the start of this experiment that could be mined for how I want to show up. I grabbed my notebook and flipped to the pages where I'd written what I'd hoped to embody by my fifty-fifth birthday.

*Vibrant, healthy glow. Deeply grounded confidence. Pride of culture and ancestors. Creative. Adventurous.* How could I use these words to inspire what I wore, what I communicated to the world?

I turned back to the first clean page in my notebook and wrote these phrases at the top of the page. Then I began to write, stream-of-consciousness, about what colors and items would embody those words for me.

I knew that I felt best in jewel tones: sapphire blues, ruby reds, emerald greens. They made me feel brighter, vibrant. Also, the colors themselves made me think of traits like depth, honesty, integrity: attributes that were core values of mine, and that I hoped I conveyed in my interactions with friends and colleagues. Some colors, like cobalt blues and rich purples, felt regal and confident, qualities to which I aspired. I researched indigo—the vibrant botanical dye that originated from

India and was brought on the Middle Passage to the Caribbean. I learned that indigo was cultivated by the enslaved Africans on Tobago, one of the two islands of my homeland. For sure all of these hues would have to be in strong rotation in my closet.

And then I thought of my progenitors, who include not just West Africans but also Indians and Chinese ancestors who came to the Caribbean as indentured laborers after slavery was abolished. I thought of the colors that are associated with West Africa, East and South Asia, as well as the Caribbean: cinnamon, curry, nutmeg, okra. There is a richness within hues of these spices, and of the land, and of the greens and blues of the Caribbean Sea. I thought of the jewelry that my grandmother had given me: silver filigree earrings from India, and gold "cocoa pod" bracelets—bangles that had details shaped like cocoa pods, and reminiscent of the *manilla* bracelets, and that were often used as currency in the transatlantic slave trade in West Africa.

I wrote all these thoughts and more in my notebook, and then when I was finished, I entered my closet. I tried on every item of clothing, and anything that was uncomfortable went into the donate pile. (Two years of working from home during the pandemic had taught me that life is too short for uncomfortable clothing, I don't care how cute it is.) Also, anything that didn't seem like it reflected what I had written in my notebook, or could be a part of an outfit that did, also went in the pile. By the end of the afternoon, I'd created a considerable stack of clothing to give away. The items that remained felt like . . . well, *me*. They seemed clearer and more reflective of the person I wanted to be. Suddenly, style felt more important than just being about the clothes.

A few years ago, I received a LinkedIn request from a woman named Karen Williams. When I clicked on her profile, I learned that she was a producer, host, and fashion model whose work focused on "empowered aging." Intrigued, I accepted her request and searched her social media accounts to learn more.

It turns out Karen had a successful modeling career years earlier as a teenager and while attending college at Brown University. She had cultivated an international profile before eventually leaving modeling to pursue filmmaking. But thirty years later, her former agent found her and asked her to return to modeling. She agreed, but decided that she could only do it if it was meaningful and centered around the concept of empowered aging. Since it is so rare to see silver-haired women in the beauty industry, I reached out to her and asked if she'd share her thoughts with me about her experiences.

Once we connected, she began. "You know, Karen, when I was younger, in some ways I was protected from the brutality of modeling, because I was also cultivating this other career at Brown," she said. "So I could see the pressures of the business, and how dangerous it could be to a young woman's self-esteem. And in many ways, because I never fully viewed modeling as an end goal, it allowed me to join in the advocacy for the inclusion of darker-skinned models and models with different body sizes. It didn't happen then, but thirty years later, we now see a lot more inclusivity."

When she was asked to return to modeling, she knew she had to approach it very intentionally, and be an integral part of the advocacy work she was doing. "My activism work has always been about diversity and inclusion, and I believe that age should also be a necessary criterion for inclusion," she told me. "So if I were going to come back to the industry after an almost thirty-year absence, I needed to be part of the conversation about what it means to be a woman of color who is embracing her silver hair. There's such a paucity of representation when it comes to age, and I wanted to be a part of that representation."

I loved what she was saying, but I couldn't help but press further. "I agree with you: the more diversity and inclusion we see in the media and the more we see ourselves reflected back to us, the more we can imagine bigger possibilities for who we are and who we can be," I said. "But Karen, you're empirically beautiful. You make a living because of your physical beauty. Not all of us look like you, and it can be more challenging for the rest of us to feel beautiful."

She smiled. "I acknowledge that I'm in an industry where it's all smoke and mirrors," she said. "There are angles and lighting and makeup artists and photographers who know how to make us look a certain way. So the physicality, to a certain extent, is a mirage. But the fact that I'm no longer in my teens or twenties is obvious, and in this industry, that's rare. And important. And the reason that I'm so comfortable in doing the work I do is because I have *never* measured myself on my physicality. I am far more acutely appreciative of things that have nothing to do with how I look. If I wasn't, as I grew older, I would be lost. It's so much more important for me—for all of us, really—to focus on what makes us *feel* beautiful."

I thought of Stasia, and her advice about tapping into how you feel as a lens for how you express yourself through clothing. Karen continued: "We *all* must do this self-interrogation. And I have to tell you, I don't necessarily feel my most beautiful when I'm fully made-up, in designer clothing. Being made to be pretty in front of a camera isn't when I feel my most beautiful. My most beautiful moments are when I am filled with purpose, passion, love. I just feel abundance. Joy. I remind myself that the center of who I am is not what I do, but who and how I love. And guess what? To me, to my mind, when I see myself filled with purpose, passion, and love, I *look* better."

"This makes sense to me," I said. "However, when people see your work, they're generally looking at two-dimensional images. Are you telling me that when you're ensuring your life is filled with purpose and passion, you can see a difference in the images from when you're not?"

"One hundred percent." She was emphatic. "*One hundred percent.* People react differently to me when I'm taking care of my spirit. *Photographers* react differently. It's not just modeling, but also every aspect of my life. And I'll be damned if anyone tells me that they can't see a difference in the final photographs, because *I* can see it. It makes such a difference. And if my work is about empowered aging, and the product of that work is made evident in images that are taken of me, it's imperative that I ensure that I'm always moving with purpose and passion."

"So how do you do that?"

"Well, I do integrative work. I'm a long-time practitioner of yoga and meditation. Part of my daily practice is asking myself every morning, 'How can I serve? How can I show up?' I find that having a spiritual practice is so essential navigating life and how I process life. I am constantly defining my beauty as something that emanates from deep inside of me. Because if I were to base it on what's on the outside, and solely on other people's perceptions of what they define as 'beautiful,' I would be in serious trouble."

Speaking with Karen and Stasia, I realized I'd held some preconceived notions of what it means to be beautiful that weren't particularly accurate. I'd always known that beauty could be, in large part, self-defined: that we could emphasize those physical attributes we were proud of and communicate their beauty. What I don't think I fully appreciated was that beauty appreciation has very little to do with *any* physical attributes. That instead, regardless of body size, or fashion-savvy, the size of a person's nose or lips or, yes, whether a person colors their hair or refuses to, what people are most attracted to is what Stasia describes as *congruency*: the confidence of showing up as who you wholly are and who you mean yourself to be. Congruency is what you feel when you can look at yourself in the mirror and think, *There I am. Who I am is clearly visible.*

But honestly, there are even bigger implications to our congruency that I hadn't considered before. I admit that even though I've always been intrigued by style, there has also been a part of me that considered clothing and appearance a somewhat frivolous concern. But of course that's not true.

For example, consider the following: as of this writing, only nineteen states in America have passed legislation prohibiting discrimination based on hair texture. Black women are 80 percent more likely than white women to agree with the statement, "I have to change my hair from its natural state in order to fit in at the office." A report published in 2020 by the Pew Research Center indicates that around the world, women experience social hostilities—that is, harassment from individuals or groups—due to clothing that is considered too religious, or not religious enough. And in Canada in the summer of 2022, Lisa LaFlamme, an award-winning newscaster with over thirty-five years of experience, was let go from her contract early, apparently over her decision to let her hair go silver during the pandemic.

If this shocks you, it shouldn't. Stories like this are so common that gerontologist and educator Jeanette Leardi was prompted to coin the term *catacombing*: "relegating to the sidelines and out of view a competent, productive woman who has consciously decided to let her personal appearance reflect her individual biological age." Even if we want to believe that how we dress, or style our hair, or even wear our jewelry really matter very little, the world keeps telling us the opposite. Our appearance, especially as we connect with our own congruency, can be *deeply* political.

For this reason, far be it from me to advocate that we all ditch the hair dye and wear whatever we want, consequences be damned. But I do believe, as Stasia and Karen suggest, it's important to interrogate ourselves about *why* we make those choices, and about what those choices say both about societal expectations and our own views about ourselves. For me, it was deeply clarifying to consider the attributes that I aim to grow into, and brainstorm how I could express those attributes through the way I dress or the way I wear my hair. As I wear more of the spice colors of my African, Chinese, and East Indian heritages, more of the blues and greens and indigo and jewel tones of my beloved Caribbean homeland, and let my hair continue to grow as big and salt-and-peppery as possible, the more often I find, when I look in the mirror, I think to myself: *there I am*. And to date, the reward of that congruency has been worth any potential risk.

So I'm clearly on my way. But Karen mentioned something that I hadn't fully explored yet: the cultivation of a solid spiritual practice that could help me navigate my present and my future. While I had certainly dabbled in various faith and spiritual practices my whole life, I hadn't found one that felt fully right yet.

Perhaps it was time.

# PART III

# Connect

# SIX

# Soul Fire

St. Joseph's Convent is one of the most venerable Catholic girls' high schools in Trinidad & Tobago. My mother attended St. Joseph's, a point of pride for her, so when I was fourteen years old and our family moved back to Trinidad after three years in Kingwood, Texas, there was no question where I'd be getting my education. My father, a non-Catholic who was raised in the Anglican faith, knew better than to argue.

Trinidad & Tobago is a country of many cultures and faiths. It was formerly a Spanish colony and then a British one. During colonial times, thanks to the labor of enslaved Africans, sugar and cocoa plantations flourished. After the British abolished slavery in 1838, the former enslavers brought Chinese, Portuguese, Indians, and others to the islands as indentured laborers, in an attempt to prop up the sugar and cocoa industries that had lost their workforce. Venezuelan farmers with experience in cacao production followed. The result? An uncommonly multiracial and multicultural population, with all the associated customs, foods, music, and religious and spiritual practices woven tightly into the fabric of the country. To this day, national holidays include not only Christian holidays but the sacred days of several other religions as well.

So while Convent was unquestionably Catholic, the school welcomed students of all cultures and faith traditions. My friends were Catholic, Anglican, Jehovah's Witness, Hindu, Muslim, and more. This wasn't strange: it seemed we all had family members—often but not always through marriage—who practiced a faith different from ours. Non-Catholics were welcome to attend any religious services our school held. They were also welcome to sit any of them out without worry of adverse consequence. It was just how we Trinis rolled.

Because my dad's new job was in rural south Trinidad, a two-and-a-half-hour drive from school, my parents made unorthodox living arrangements for me. During the week I would stay in town with my maternal grandparents so I could attend Convent, and on weekends I would return home to my parents and younger sister.

My grandparents lived in a rambling brick house in Goodwood Park, a suburban neighborhood of the capital city of Port-of-Spain, located in the foothills of Trinidad's northern mountain range. Their home was surrounded by a sprawling, manicured garden that exploded with tropical flowers, and from the front step, you could catch a tiny glimpse of the Gulf of Paria in the distance. Despite not actually being oceanfront, the house was cooled by the sea breeze that was constantly rustling the leaves of the fruit trees that surrounded the property.

The house was filled with keepsakes from their travels: threadbare Persian rugs, blue and white Delft pottery, and batik throw pillows from various Caribbean islands. My grandparents had separate bedrooms, but they were connected by a door that was always left ajar. At night when the lights were off, I would hear them calling to each other, telling each other jokes until they fell asleep. My grandfather's bedroom was decidedly masculine, smelling of leather and pipe tobacco, while my grandmother's bedroom was a monument to femininity if ever there was one. The antique mahogany table was covered with embroidered linens she had made, and sitting on top of the cloths were scores of ornate perfume bottles, vials of mysterious face creams and powders, and a huge jewelry case that, when opened, featured a tiny plastic ballerina who turned wonkily in time with its music box—the Henry Mancini "Love Story" theme.

But all these items were dwarfed by a huge Sacred Heart statue placed in the middle of the table: a blond, blue-eyed, peaceful-looking Jesus stood with a flaming heart encircled by a crown of thorns embedded in his breast. On the other side of the room, on my grandmother's chest of drawers, a large porcelain figure of the Virgin Mary loomed, arms outstretched and inviting, her bare feet standing on a serpent, just visible under her robes.

Every day after school, I would shed the aqua blue skirt and white blouse of my uniform, put on shorts and a t-shirt, and keep my grandmother company in her bedroom. She spent a lot of time in the rocking chair at the foot of her bed, sometimes crocheting, sometimes doing a crossword puzzle, sometimes reading the devotional booklet she had gotten at Sunday mass. I would sit on the bench in front of her dressing table, and if I was patient, she would tell me stories of when my mother, my aunt, and my uncle were little. And she would always give me advice.

"Karen, you must always pray to Jesus," she would say. "Even when you leave Convent and go out into the world. He will always help you."

"Yes, Granny," I would nod.

"Don't let me find out you workin' obeah, now," she would giggle, her round belly bouncing as she laughed at her own joke. I'd laugh, too. "Obeah" is the word Trinis use for a mystical system of practices that outsiders called "voodoo." For Catholics like our family, the word conjured up frightening images of hexes and dark sorcery.

One day, I grew serious. "Granny," I asked, "is there really obeah in Trinidad?"

"I don't think so," she answered. "Not anymore. But when I was a little girl," she said, her voice lowering, "I used to hear the drums in the hills behind my house."

A shiver of delight ran down my spine. I was entranced: drums in the rainforest hills seemed far more exciting than the hymns we sang during Convent mass. But I didn't dare ask any more questions. Even though my grandmother disapproved of obeah, it was clear by her tone that she held a certain respect for this mysterious spiritual practice. Asking anything further would have been impolite.

When I was in my mid-twenties, life was challenging: I had just endured the singular hell that is taking and passing the Texas bar exam; my first marriage was ending; and I had been laid off from my first lawyer job. My savings were rapidly dwindling. For the first time in my life, I struggled to get out of bed. As I had promised my grandmother years earlier, I continued to pray. I hadn't been a regular churchgoer for years, but when I tried returning to the Catholic church, I found that the ritual of the mass wasn't comforting. Instead, the formal language full of "thee" and "thou" rang hollow. What was it we were actually saying in the service, anyway? Was anyone listening? Was religion pointless? Was faith? What was our purpose on this planet, anyway?

Because of the pluralistic religious culture of my childhood, I decided to do a bit of research. I began reading. *A lot*. I read books like *The History of God*, written by Karen Armstrong, a former nun. It's a treatise on the way the three dominant monotheistic religions—Judaism, Christianity, and Islam—shaped the world's perception of God. I read *Autobiography of a Yogi* by Paramahansa Yogananda, a thorough introduction to the East Asian practice of yoga, and considered one of the top one hundred spiritual books of the twentieth century. I read *Living Buddha, Living Christ*, an exploration of the synchronicities in the teachings of both the Buddha and Jesus Christ, written by Thich Nhat Hanh, a Vietnamese monk, global spiritual leader, peace activist, and poet.

After reading and reading, even though I still wasn't sure where I stood with Catholicism, all the books I consumed helped convince me that a spiritual practice—of whatever kind—was a powerful way to help navigate life. I remembered my non-Catholic classmates at Convent: my Hindu friends lighting the *deyas* on their houses for Diwali, and my Muslim friends excitedly discussing their mothers making *sawine* for dessert to celebrate the end of Ramadan on Eid. I understood more the gifts of joy and connection that their own practices brought to their lives, just as celebrating Christmas and praying the Rosary brought to my grandmother and my mother.

And so, tentatively, I attempted a few tiny spiritual practices to see if they brought me any more comfort.

First, I began a gratitude practice, reinvigorating an element of my childhood evening prayers by taking a moment every night to think of one good thing that happened during the day. Admittedly, in those early days, the only good thing I might have been able to think of was my perfectly boiled egg for breakfast. Still, it counted. Each time I could come up with some-thing—and blessedly I did, every night—I felt a little bit better.

Second, I tried meditating. I was never sure if I did it right, since within seconds my mind would wander. But even so, I realized that simply sitting for a few minutes every day and slowing my breath made me feel better. Eventually I was sitting in stillness every morning for thirty minutes. Even my mother remarked: "You seem calmer. What are you doing?" When I told her, she was skeptical, as meditation wasn't commonly spoken of in the Catholic church at the time. But since there was no denying that I was slowly coming out of my funk, she decided to just be grateful I'd found a practice that helped. Life happened, and I fell out of my meditation practice but not my gratitude practice—by the time I became a mother, I'd had a gratitude practice for years. Still, I was unsure about how to raise my daughter to cultivate her own faith, so I decided to fall back on what was familiar from my childhood: religion. Alexis was baptized in the Episcopal church, the American arm of the Anglican church. On learning that Alex would be baptized Episcopalian, my father smiled but, again, wisely said nothing. My mother was also quiet—I'm sure she would have preferred that Alex be raised Catholic—but at that point, I think she was relieved that Alex was going to be a member of *any* church.

Alex thrived at Holy Spirit Episcopal. She became an acolyte, dutifully donning white robes and assisting the priest during Sunday services. Later she became a counselor at an Episcopal summer camp in the Piney Woods of Texas. She even, for one fleeting moment, considered becoming a priest. As Alex headed off to college to study visual communication design, I didn't know if or how her own spiritual practice would continue or grow, but I'm confident that her childhood has given her some grounded faith-based understanding, should she become curious about her own spirituality in the future.

Her flying the nest, of course, left me with more space and time to consider my own spirituality. Now that I wasn't responsible for raising a young one anymore, I realized that in my efforts to ensure the spiritual formation of my daughter, I had forgotten about my own soul care. Religious practice wasn't exactly what I was looking for, since my desire wasn't about the external experience of connecting with a faith community. Instead, I hoped to create something that was more internally focused. In the same way that I'd reignited my pilot light, I wanted to address my spiritual health—to tend my soul fire. The call to return to my own spiritual caretaking had become persistent.

There's some science behind why we seek spiritual comfort. In her book *The Awakened Brain: The New Science of Spirituality and Our Quest for an Inspired Life*, Columbia University professor and psychologist Dr. Lisa Miller writes, "Whether or not we participate in a spiritual practice or adhere to a faith tradition, whether or not we identify as religious or spiritual, our brain has a natural inclination toward and a docking station for spiritual awareness." She continues: "Just as we are cognitive, physical and emotional beings, we are also spiritual beings. In other words, it's possible that we are built to be spiritual and that spirituality might be a fundamental and necessary part of our human inheritance that contributes to our mental health." So it doesn't matter what faith community we call home—or if we haven't got one at all. We are wired to seek connection with something bigger than us. We are healthier when we cultivate our awareness of a sacred, interconnected world.

As it happens, evidence also suggests that meditation, prayer, and other spiritual practices may have significant impacts on our memory, cognition, mood, and overall mental health as we get older. Dr. Andrew Newberg, the director of research at the Jefferson-Myrna Brind Center of Integrative Medicine at Thomas Jefferson University, says that research shows that "meditation practice and increased mindfulness are related to improved attention functions and cognitive flexibility," adding "this may have the most important implications for aging."

So it seemed like this was the perfect time for me to do a bit of soul-searching. As I considered my options, I wanted to focus on simple habits I could include in my life that would ensure that I was checking in with myself and "tuning in" to the sacred in a consistent way. But unlike when I was younger, I also wanted these practices to draw upon the fullness of who I am now: a once-Catholic-now-Episcopalian-Caribbean-immigrant-descended-from-enslaved-Africans-and-Chinese-and-Indian-indentured-laborers. I wanted the ways in which I connected with the sacred to be informed by the totality of my history and culture, rooted in my values and ethics. And I wanted to do it in a way that felt inclusive and expansive.

No biggie, right?

I mentioned this wish list to my friend A'Driane, thinking that she would laugh at such a tall order, but she didn't even blink. "You need to meet my friend Tuhina," she said without hesitation. "She's the perfect person to get you started."

Tuhina Verma Rasche is an ordained Lutheran minister who has, in her own words, "a complicated relationship with Jesus." She is a second-generation Indian American woman who was raised in a devout Hindu household. Scanning her bio, I learned her work focuses on both dismantling white supremacy and conversations on the complexities of identities . . . and honestly, at that point, I stopped reading. She sounded like *exactly* who I needed to speak with, so I asked A'Driane to make an introduction.

When I met Tuhina, she was fresh off a cross-country relocation and starting a new job at the Aspen Institute, an organization that gathers diverse, nonpartisan thought leaders, creatives, scholars, and others to address some of the world's most complex problems. I explained to her why I was so keen that we meet. "I'm really interested in how your former Hindu faith might frame some of your current Christian spiritual practice," I explained. "But let's first start with this: What was the best part of growing up Hindu?"

"I first really began to understand that being Hindu was something I should celebrate around the time I was nine years old," she told me. "I grew up in Colorado, but my family and I had gone to India for about a month to the village where my parents grew up. We went during the festival of Durga Puja, which is the celebration of good overcoming evil. Durga is a goddess of war: a woman with eight arms who rides a tiger, a warrior who defeats the powers of evil. Every night we would put on our best clothes and go to the center of the village to hear the conch-shell-blowing contests that were the call to worship. It was the first time I had experienced true celebration in community, since there weren't a lot of Hindus in Denver, Colorado, in the 1980s. I was so taken by it that I asked my grandmother to buy me a conch shell designed for the call. It was my awakening to the realization that, wow, women can be badasses too."

"I love this," I said. "Given that you clearly are proud of having grown up Hindu, *and* you're currently a Lutheran pastor, do you feel the need to reconcile these two important parts of your life?"

"It has taken years for me to answer this question. I actually don't know that they *have* to be reconciled," she said. "My Hinduism and my Christianity don't have to meld together, but they can simply *be* together. As a Christian pastor, God sings in my bones in Lutheran theology: I can't turn that off. But at the same time, I can't lobotomize the practices and traditions that I grow up with. So they exist together.

"For example—and this is a strange thing for a pastor to admit—what I learned from my family is that you don't have to go to church. Of course, when we could, we would go to puja, the Hindu worship ritual, and be among people and with our community. But at the same time, I grew up having a home altar, where I witnessed my parents praying and where my brother and I were encouraged to pray. So I was raised knowing that God was in my home: we didn't have to go anywhere to meet with God. This was confirmed when we were in India and I saw roadside altars to deities. So just like a church is a sanctuary and a sacred place, I know from my childhood that sanctuaries and sacred places can be anywhere and everywhere."

"And honestly," she continued, "that's the thing I'm so excited about as I'm getting older: I'm interrogating what it means for my faith life to continue to ripple outward and expand. As an immigrant daughter, I hadn't been allowed to take up space. As a brown woman, I'm not supposed to take up space. But now, in my spiritual practice, I interrogate myself on what it means to take up space, so that I can inhale and exhale fully, and deeply."

This was exactly what I was hoping for myself, and I wondered how she was making this happen. How did she integrate the practices of two different spiritual faiths without betraying the integrity of either doctrine? What did that interrogation look like for her, practically speaking?

Her answer surprised me with its simplicity: she told me that writing was essential for connecting with her own inner wisdom, and that she starts and ends her day writing longhand in her journal. She added that she also does a lot of mindful walking. "I believe it's important for my spiritual health to be in relationship with God's creation," Tuhina said. "Part of taking up space in the world is acknowledging the world and having the world acknowledge you back. So when I walk, I am mindful of the steps I take, and the birdsong and the wind in the trees. I'm mindful of my breath and being intentional about the space I'm taking up as I walk. It's a spiritual practice."

I asked Tuhina what other advice she would give to someone beginning a spiritual practice for the first time. She thought for a moment. "For me, the most important part of coming into my own spiritual awareness was connecting with myself and acknowledging myself," she said. "I needed to learn to acknowledge my own spirit, so I could prove to myself that I was worthy of spiritual practices, and then I could be open to spiritual practices. And as I said, the best way I've found to do this was to journal. Sometimes I would write just a record of my day. There were times when I was really struggling, and I would just write something to prove that I exist. That I was alive."

Tuhina's words—that to begin a spiritual practice, you should first connect with yourself—felt important. I already had a thriving journaling practice, and it was effective in helping me process questions or challenges I wrestled with in my day-to-day life. But I used my notebook as more of a cerebral tool than a spiritual one, and the practice was beginning to feel somewhat rote. And it wasn't lost on me that Tuhina was the latest of several folks I'd spoken to for whom "expansion" or "taking up space" was a mantra. Perhaps the recurrence of this theme was a signal that it was time to expand the way I approached my writing. Perhaps it was time to explore how I could connect with the sacred more meaningfully in its pages. How could I create the space to go deep into self-inquiry and self-interrogation?

My friend Giyen Kim immediately came to mind. We've known each other for years, and I knew that she had been on sabbatical for the past few months. This wasn't her first, either. But unlike an academic sabbatical, where an institution pays for a tenured professor to leave their daily duties to do special research and writing, Giyen's sabbaticals were self-funded personal retreats. During many of her previous sabbaticals, she had been a single parent and the sole financial support to her only child, and so I knew that her times away from work must have been a significant sacrifice to her little family. But she used them to help ground herself and clarify next steps for her own life and her life as a parent. Now that her child is an adult, I'm sure these periods of rest feel less risky. And she always seemed to make all she could of these times away, using them for travel, rest, and reflection. I decided to ask Giyen about her philosophy around sabbatical, so when she returned from her most recent trip, I reached out.

"So how do you know it's time to take one?" I asked Giyen, after we'd caught up on each other's families and lives. "Is there anything formal about how you make the decision to go on sabbatical?"

"I took each of my four sabbaticals because there was a big change in my life," Giyen told me. "I needed to both process the grief associated with that change and figure out what I needed to do next. I tend to take sabbaticals when I'm in transition."

With Alex leaving for college, my milestone birthday, and our milestone wedding anniversary—well, this certainly was a time of transition. I listened closely.

"For example, the morning my father died," Giyen was saying, "I got the call right before the start of a benefit banquet I'd been organizing for months, and after I hung up, I continued working. I had just learned my dad died, and *I kept working*. Later that day when I got home, I realized my refusal to stop was a sign that I needed a recalibration."

Giyen and her father had a complicated relationship. The grief around his death wasn't so much about losing a formidable presence in her life as it was about letting go of any hope for reconciliation. "When I spoke with my good friend Mandy, she said, 'You need to go on a ten-day silent meditation retreat, to process your grief, and to center yourself again.' She'd told me about this retreat for years, and I finally listened."

"Whoa!" I stopped her. "Ten days of not speaking?!"

"The 'not speaking' was the easiest part, to be honest," she said. "The hard part was the physical pain of sitting on a pad for ten hours a day, meditating."

My eyes widened. "You're going to have to walk me through this."

"It was Vipassanā meditation, which is just breath work. There are no mantras." Vipassanā, I later learned, is a Buddhist term often translated as "insight." "I shared a room with one person, and we would get up at five in the morning for our first meditation at 5:30 a.m. We were only served breakfast and lunch, with no dinner. And we were completely silent."

"This sounds really intense."

"It *was* intense. We meditated for ten to eleven hours every day, with meal breaks, and a walking break for about an hour, but that was it. In addition to not speaking, we weren't allowed to read, or journal, or anything else. Not everyone made it—a few people left after a couple of days. By day five or six, you finally get to a place where you've run through all the lists in your head. You've had all the dark thoughts, and you've had all the happy thoughts. And then finally, you arrive at a point where you just surrender to the present moment. And the surrendering is unbelievably transformational. Your mind suddenly becomes very clear."

Giyen described the shift she experienced between the day of her arrival and when she left. "When I first walked into the meditation center, I thought I had made a stupid mistake by signing up for the retreat. I was still in grief and I felt adrift. But by the end of the ten days, I was just feeling pure joy, from deep inside of me. On the final night, we were allowed to speak with each other about our experiences, having been through this really powerful time together. And we were all filled with this sense of peace. It was incredible. I left making myself the promise that I was going to meditate an hour every day for the rest of my life. Of course, I didn't manage to keep up that schedule, but still: I'll never forget that feeling, and I know I can always find that place again. That knowledge is unbelievably reassuring to me."

I stared at Giyen in wonder and perhaps a bit of envy. "This sounds really amazing, Giyen," I said.

"I'd love to take the kinds of sabbaticals you do, with months off at a time, or even a few days at a meditation center—although I'm not sure I could handle ten days of silence without a journal or a book. But I don't know how I'd ever be able to check out of my life and my responsibilities for an extended time."

"Look," said Giyen, "I know that my story, with my multiple sabbaticals, isn't particularly relatable, and I tell people all the time what a tremendous amount of privilege I have to be able to do the things that I'm doing, even though I sacrifice a lot to do them. I would never tell anyone to make the same choices that I do. But I do believe that we all can and should go on a journey of self-knowledge, and that journey can simply start with asking ourselves 'What do I want to do today?' You don't have to ask yourself that question every day, but if you're not asking yourself that question *at all*, then you're not giving back to yourself in a way that you deserve. I think everyone needs to take the time to examine themselves. It's where we begin to discover our meaning and purpose and our interconnectedness with the wider world."

I couldn't agree with Giyen more. In fact, for years my daily journaling practice has included three prompts: *How can I feel healthy today? How can I feel connected today? How can I feel purposeful today?* And then I add the answers to these questions to my daily to-do list. I love how open-ended the questions are, inviting me to be creative as I answer them, and doing them daily ensures that I have a cadence of checking in with myself, in the manner that Giyen suggests.

But still, I was intrigued with the idea of taking a break from my life for focused introspection. So while Giyen's ten-day meditation retreat felt extreme, I wondered what it might look like to go off the grid for a couple of days. I did a little online research, and then I called Marcus at work. "Hey," I said when he answered. "How would you feel if I left tomorrow to spend a couple of days in the woods?"

You need to know that although Marcus is an avid camper, I am decidedly not. He once told me, early in our relationship, that our marriage wouldn't be a success until he witnessed me with a shovel over my left shoulder and biodegradable toilet paper under my right arm, walking into the woods while whistling. It's been twenty years, and by his definition, our marriage is still not a success. But as I've told him repeatedly, my mom and dad sent me to university in the hope that I'd never have to sleep on the ground. The way I see it, camping would just be disrespectful to my parents.

Needless to say, when I called him to let him know I was planning to spend some time in the forest for a couple of days, he was stunned, until I assured him that I had no plans to spend any of that time in a tent. "I found a place to camp that has little cabins in the woods," I said, sending him the link.

"Wait, it says here that each cabin has air conditioning and a private bathroom. This isn't even close to camping."

"I beg to differ," I said. "You'll notice there is no Wi-Fi. If that's not roughing it, Sporto, then I do not know what is."

"Jesus."

"So I'm going to go bivouac in the woods for a couple of days," I said.

"You're going to do what, now?"

"You know, be alone with my thoughts. Live the ascetic life."

"I don't think two days in a cabin that provides a full kitchen and ingredients for s'mores is 'the ascetic life.'"

"It is for me."

And so the next day, I headed out of town for forty-eight hours on my own. Even though I feigned confidence with Marcus, I was nervous: I knew that the cabins would be comfortable, but it had been a long time since I'd traveled by myself. The idea of being alone with my thoughts without the internet to surf felt really isolating. And as I turned my car onto the gravel road into the site, I wondered if I was really capable of doing this.

*SLOW DOWN*, read a sign as I drove past.

*That's what I'm here for*, I thought to myself.

After about five minutes, I arrived at the campsite and parked next to a circle of stones for building a small campfire. Texas was experiencing a severe drought and there was a burn ban in effect, so I had no plans for lighting one. The summer heat would have made a fire unbearable, anyway. I walked up the steps and keyed in the code to unlock the cabin. The interior was cozy, with a queen-sized platform bed, clean linens, a tiny kitchenette with a cheery candy-apple-red mini fridge, and a little bathroom with a toilet and shower. And thankfully, the air conditioner was pumping out cool air. *This will be perfect*, I thought to myself, trying to put the image of Marcus rolling his eyes out of my mind.

Unpacking was quick and easy. After that, I surveyed my home for the next couple of days, and for the first time saw a little notecard I hadn't noticed before on the table. On it was written helpful instructions about what to do if I came in contact with a wild boar ("don't go near it"), and how to avoid cottonmouth and rattlesnake bites ("wear long pants and ankle boots in the woods"). *Good thing I'm never leaving this cabin*, I thought as I hooked up my little portable Bluetooth speaker. Music now on, I began making myself an early dinner: sauteed vegetables and pasta. Simple.

After dinner, it was still light outside, so I decided to grab my camera and risk a walk through the campground. If I stayed in the middle of the gravel road, I assumed the likelihood of running into something that could eat me would be reduced, and I'd be back in my safe little cabin before dark. I walked out, taking my phone with me for potential 9-1-1 dialing purposes.

I began my trek at a considerable clip, taking photographs of the sun through the foliage, the tree-lined gravel road, the occasional wildflower. As I walked, I passed more cabins, tucked into the woods, each with their own names: *Refugio. Setsuko. Paulette. Carma.* (Mine was *Ramón.*) I had read on the website that the cabins were named after the grandparents of the company's team members and guests. I smiled.

Up ahead, there was a sign nailed to one of the trees. I squinted to make it out as I approached.

*KAREN.*

I looked around the area. Unlike the other cabins I'd passed, there weren't any cars parked outside. It appeared empty. *I guess someone's grandmother had my name*, I thought; *That's kinda cool.* I took a photo of the sign, and then picked up a small smooth stone in front of the cabin as a memento. I returned to the gravel road. About forty feet later, another sign appeared.

*SLOW DOWN.*

Message received. I slowed my pace. I walked for another half mile, more slowly, taking more photographs. And then I turned back toward my own cabin.

Finally inside, I put my camera down, wondering what I could do next. I turned the music back on and put the kettle on the stove for a cup of tea.

And then, suddenly, the power went out. The stove turned off, the air conditioner stopped its hum, and the lights illuminating the increasingly dark cabin extinguished.

I called Marcus. "The power is out," I said.

"Oh no," he replied. "Is it the whole campground, or just you?"

"I have no idea. I don't know what to do."

I could hear him tapping on his computer keyboard. "It looks like it's the whole county."

"Marcus, I can't stay here with the power out."

"I know."

"It's over a hundred degrees outside. This cabin is going to turn into an oven."

"I know."

"I think it's getting warmer already."

"I'm sure."

"What should I do?"

Marcus breathed deeply. "Of course you could come home if you want to," he said. "But I think you should give it some time. I mean, you've already paid for two nights, and the sun is already going down, so the worst of the day's heat is over. Maybe it'll come back on soon."

"I guess so."

"I'm going to hang up now," he said. "You shouldn't use your phone, so you can save the charge. I'll text you later to check on you."

"Okay." I hung up the phone. The air in the cabin was getting warmer, and I looked around, trying to figure out what to do next. I poured myself some cold water from the fridge, and sat on the bed. I tried not to freak out. The light in the cabin was dimming. Soon I would be in total darkness, so even reading or writing would be out of the question.

*KAREN.* The image of the black-and-white signs on the gravel road filled my mind. *SLOW DOWN.*

*I guess I could meditate,* I thought. It had been a while. But I climbed on the bed, and sat cross-legged in front of the large picture window looking out to the woods. I closed my eyes, and slowed my breath. *Slow down.*

As I sat, I noticed that my shoulders were tense, so I willed myself to relax them. Gradually, they dropped. I became aware of the noises outside of the cabin: the breeze rustling through the trees, the call of a distant bird.

*Slow down.*

The air in the cabin didn't feel as warm anymore. In fact, it felt comfortable. Was that possible?

*Slow down.*

I sat like that for about twenty minutes, until my phone buzzed. It was a text from Marcus: "Is the power still out?"

"Yes, but I'm okay," I responded. I tossed the phone aside and returned to my slow breathing.

About twenty minutes later, the power returned and the air conditioner roared to life. Startled, I opened my eyes to the bright cabin lights. *Had it been that loud before?* I wondered.

I made my tea. That short meditation session had shifted something inside me: Despite my initial fear of being in the woods by myself, I was calm and relaxed. That night, I slept like a baby. The next day, and for the remainder of my time in the woods, I alternated between writing in my journal, reading my books, and meditating in silence.

On the drive back to my house, I promised myself that I would begin a daily meditation practice—perhaps just fifteen minutes, perhaps just to start my day, before climbing out of bed. The simple slowing and checking in with myself was restful. It was calming. *Karen, slow down.* Why wouldn't I want to start my days this way?

My friend Attillah Springer is an essayist and documentarian from my homeland of Trinidad. A few weeks after returning from my micro-sabbatical, I read this sentence on her blog: "'Obeah' was used as a general term that lumped together all African spiritual practice, and anything else that could be vaguely construed as a threat against colonial authorities."

As I read her words, a question dawned on me: Could it be that obeah, which I had always assumed was some sort of dark magic, was simply the name for indigenous spiritual practices that enslaved Africans brought with them on the Middle Passage? Was it possible that in my suspicion of the practice, I had fallen for colonialist propaganda?

This certainly seemed to be the case. For over four hundred years between the fifteenth and nineteenth centuries, more than fifteen million men, women, and children were abducted from West Africa and sold into forced labor in the transatlantic slave trade. While these enslaved Africans were stolen from their homes, families, and communities, they brought elements of their homeland with them, including their indigenous Yoruba spiritual practices. Because of this, their culture and religion tended to be the primary influence over the subculture of the societies of the enslaved. And as Attillah states, these spiritual practices were viewed with deep suspicion by the European colonists. In Trinidad, the practices evolved into a religion known as Trinidad Orisha (also informally and locally known as *Shango*). Today's Trinidad Orisha practices include not only those from Yoruba traditions but also elements of Catholicism, Hinduism, and Kabbalah. A marked element of Trinidad Orisha practice is call-and-response singing, accompanied by drumming—likely the music my grandmother had heard in the rainforest hills behind her house when she was a little girl.

As I'd begun this exploration of my own spirituality, one of my intentions was to research the faith practices of my ancestors, especially if it meant interrogating my own colonialist thinking. As it happens, Attillah is a devotee of Trinidad Orisha, and I realized that she'd be the perfect person to teach me about the faith of my enslaved forebears. I contacted her and asked if she would mind telling me more about what Trinidad Orisha is, how it relates to obeah, and just generally set me straight. She happily agreed, and one day we sat for two hours catching up, me from my Houston living room, and her on her porch in Trinidad.

"Were you always a practitioner of Orisha?" I asked her.

"Well, sort of," she answered. "My grandmother was a very good Catholic woman who was in the habit of giving us bush baths."

I laughed. If your grandmother insists you need a bush bath, something has likely gone terribly wrong. A "bush bath" is a ritual of pouring water that has been infused with local herbs, plants, or flowers over the body, which, according to ancestral tradition, will wash away illness, bad luck, or even evil spirits.

"So on one hand, I used to go to mass with my grandmother at Mount Saint Benedict Abbey. On the other, she would remind me that if I were ever to pick a fruit from a plant after a certain hour, then I should speak to the plant, apologize to it for waking it up, and express gratitude for allowing me to take the fruit."

"Kind of a combination of two faiths, then," I said.

"Well, this wasn't unusual, right? Remember, anything not sanctioned by the church or the state during colonial times was considered obeah. And so this is where syncretism comes in: the conscious masking of Orisha divinities with Catholic saints. So there was a synthesis of African religions and Christianity, in a lot of ways, so that the enslaved would be able to continue practicing their faiths."

"I mean, think about it," she continued. "During the times of enslavement, Christianity was often used as a form of state control—a way to keep the enslaved in line. But that didn't mean that Africans simply abandoned their practices. These were the practices of people who observe nature. These were people who were in touch with their dreams, and understood that everything has an energy, a life force. So, for example, if your child gets ill in the middle of the night, what are you going to do? Would you use the practices of a new religion, Christianity, the religion of the people who held you in bondage? Or would you refer to the bank of stories that you have from your grandparents and that they have from their grandparents? You're going to pick the leaves of a herb that you know will help ease your child's suffering, until you get to a doctor. You're going to pray in the way that you know has brought your family comfort for generations."

"That makes sense," I nodded. "But you mentioned that your family was Catholic. Do you still practice Catholicism? Or do you practice a hybrid of both Catholicism and Orisha?"

"Well, I was fully initiated into Orisha in 2002, so just Orisha now," she said.

"And what does that look like? What are some of the day-to-day practices that you have that you would attribute to Orisha as opposed to any other faith tradition?"

"Well," Attillah spoke slowly. "One of the first things I do when I wake up is pour a little water on the Earth and say, 'To the Mother Earth, as I walk on you today, keep me safe. I'm going to try to tread as gently as I possibly can.' And there's also a prayer that I say, that asks for 'cool head, cool tongue, cool path,' helping me to keep my cool, essential for helping to manage my energy through the day."

"The other really important thing," she continued, "is calling the names of all the ancestors you know, and appeal to them and the energy of the Universe to keep you safe, keep you from doing harm to others, and keep you from doing harm to yourself. Because it's easy for us to be self-sabotaging and keep ourselves from our mission. So you ask for your ancestors to help guide you."

"This sounds very intention-setting," I said.

"Exactly," she smiled.

My conversations with Tuhina, Giyen, and Attillah had certainly expanded my understanding of all the ways spirituality can be experienced. From Tuhina, I learned that everywhere and anywhere can be a sacred space—even a rapidly warming cabin in the middle of the Piney Woods during the height of a brutal Texas summer. Giyen taught me that self-interrogation is important, and that daily meditation, even if it's only for fifteen minutes a day, is a good way to enhance how I check in with myself. Attillah inspired me to work a little obeah by adding an intention-setting practice involving calling on my ancestors for their guidance. (I'll probably end up calling on my grandmother, even though she warned me about practicing obeah . . . sorry, Gran!)

But the biggest lesson that I learned is that it's possible to uncouple spiritual *belief* and spiritual *practice*, and that *practice* can support *belief*. And maybe that's what we're *all* called to do: not merely *believe* in God or a higher power or the Universe or the interconnectedness of humanity but also put some intention behind a practice that helps us connect with the sacred miracle that is life. In the end, I'll likely remain a member of Holy Spirit Episcopal. But as an Afro-Caribbean woman of mixed heritage, I find it important to learn from my history and my culture and experiment with the ways they might ground me in a daily practice of my faith.

But despite my hope to solely focus on an internal spiritual practice, Tuhina stressed that it's also important to be in connection and celebration with other people. I'm a confirmed introvert, so being in community can sometimes be a challenge for me; yet I know that as I get older, community and connection will become ever more important. How can I begin to nurture meaningful connections when it doesn't come easily to me?

It was time to find out.

# SEVEN

# Radiant Alliance

It was late summer, and I was in the south of France. This sounds far more glamorous than it actually was, although admittedly no less wonderful. It all began a month earlier when my next-door neighbor Pam knocked on my door. At the time, I was living alone in a small apartment complex outside of Houston, and she and I had become friends. When I invited her in, she didn't even say hello. "You're coming with me and my cousin Kim to Europe," she said. Pam was a travel agent, and she had found some great deals. "We'll fly to Paris for a couple of days, take the train to Avignon for two days, and then the train to Barcelona for the final two days before coming home. Are you in?"

The invitation came out of the blue, but it wasn't a hard sell. The previous years had been intense: After law school graduation came the bar exam, followed quickly by divorce, before getting laid off. But I had finally gotten my feet under me, landing a good-paying job that I enjoyed and developing confidence and contentment with being on my own. It was, I felt, time to celebrate. "Yes, please," I said without hesitation. "When do we leave?"

So, there we were, three single women in a place that seemed out of a fairy tale. Avignon is a charming medieval town known especially for its stone buildings, cobblestone streets, and enchanting architecture. The town is anchored by the famed Palais des Papes, or "Palace of the Popes." In the fourteenth century, there was a split in the Catholic church called the "Papal Schism," when bishops in both Avignon and Rome claimed to be the true pope. For almost seventy years, the ones who lived in Avignon resided in the imposing *palais*, the largest gothic palace in the world.

We'd arrived in town in the late afternoon, checking into a small, locally run inn that was simple, clean, and had a large bedroom with three twin-sized beds and a private bathroom. We dropped our bags in the room, surveying our new home for the next couple of days. But relaxing would have to wait. We hadn't eaten for hours, so we washed our faces and changed our clothes. Twenty minutes later we were back outside in search of dinner, just as the sun was turning golden.

As we wandered down the cobblestone streets, we passed a small open-air market with folks selling handmade goods. We had stopped to admire their wares when we noticed a young man motioning us over to his stall, displaying rings and pendants made of silver and inlaid stone. We walked over to take a look.

"Are you from America?" He had a warm grin and a shock of jet-black hair. But his accent wasn't French.

"Yes," I said, "but you're not local, either. Where are you from?"

"Peru." He grinned wider. "Welcome to Avignon!"

We spoke for a few minutes. His name was Miguel, and his English was broken, but solid. I tried my high school Spanish on him, and his smile grew so big, I thought it might hurt his face. We complimented his handiwork, and he recommended which of the many sidewalk cafés had the best food. He was pleasant and friendly. As we made our goodbyes, he said, "After dinner, you should come back and join me. I'll be done here in a couple of hours, and I'll show you the town."

Before I could demur, Pam answered. "Okay! We'll see you then!"

As we turned away, I whispered, "Pam, are you sure this is a good idea? We don't know this man from Adam."

She made a face. "It'll be fine," she said. "There are three of us, and one of him. What could go wrong?"

We found the café that Miguel had suggested, and he was right—the food was delicious. I had my first *salade niçoise* that night and loved it so much, I ordered it several more times over the next two days. Finally relaxed and full, we paid our bill and got up from the table. By now, night had fallen.

"Let's go find Miguel!" said Pam.

"So we're really gonna do this, huh?" I looked at her like she'd grown a second head.

"Yes, we're really going to do this," she said, linking her arms in Kim's and mine. "When's the next time we're going to be in Avignon, getting shown around by a wild-haired Peruvian? Let's go."

I shot Kim a look behind Pam's back as she dragged us toward the market. When we arrived at Miguel's stall, he was packing up. "You came!" he shouted gleefully. "These are my friends!" Standing next to Miguel were two men and a woman. One of the men also looked South American, sharing the same long, wavy black hair that Miguel had. The other man and woman were French, and they were smoking cigarettes. The French-man was carrying a guitar case. They smiled their hellos.

So much for three against one. *This is how we die,* I thought, forcing a smile and shaking their hands. *No way that guitar case doesn't have a gun in it.*

Miguel finished packing his stall. "Shall we go?" The six of us followed him into the night.

After a few minutes of walking, we arrived at the Palais des Papes. "How about here?" Miguel said, as he leaned against the stone wall and slid to the ground. His friends followed suit. Pam, Kim, and I looked at each other, and joined them. The Frenchman opened his guitar case, and I cringed, anticipating our impending murders.

To my surprise, inside his case was a well-loved guitar. He pulled it out. "Sing?" He motioned in my direction.

"Me?" I stammered. "Sing what?"

He began strumming and bellowing. *"And she's biiiiiii-ying a steeee-why to haaaah-ven!"*

Pam, Kim, and I burst into laughter. Apparently, every guitarist in the world learns how to play Led Zeppelin.

Bottles of red wine and plastic cups appeared out of nowhere, and for the rest of the night the seven of us sat against the wall of the Palais des Papes, singing and laughing. They tried to teach us French folk songs. We taught them the correct pronunciation of the lyrics to John Denver's "Take Me Home, Country Roads." We shared stories and told each other jokes. The amazing thing is that we couldn't communicate in the same language: Pam and Kim didn't speak anything but English, I had my secondary school Spanish and French, and Miguel spoke Spanish, English, and very broken French. His Peruvian friend spoke Spanish and French fluently, and the Frenchman and his girlfriend only spoke French. And yet the language barriers provided very little obstacle: If Pam or Kim said anything that the others didn't understand, I would translate to Spanish, and Miguel and his friend would translate for the French speakers. If the French folks said anything we didn't understand, the Peruvians would translate back to us. Our reactions rippled out of us like a stadium wave at a sporting event, as one by one each of us understood the translations and looked directly into the eyes of the speaker as we laughed or nodded, hoping that our expressions conveyed the appreciation that our difficulty with their language couldn't.

So it went for the entire night, until the sun started peeking over the horizon. Finally, Pam, Kim, and I stood up. "We have to get some sleep," I said. "But, Miguel, thank you. This has been *amazing*." We all shared joyful hugs with each other, bidding each other farewell in three different languages. Then, filled to the brim with happiness, my travel companions and I blearily made our way back to our hotel.

We never saw Miguel and his friends again. Still, more than twenty-five years later, that night remains one of the fondest memories of my life. What the seven of us created by being open and curious and generous with each other, despite our differences and language barriers (and lubricated by wine and song, it must be said) was—well, it was nothing short of alchemy. And it was a dazzling example of our human instinct for connection.

Dr. Vivek Murthy has written extensively about the power of social connection. A physician who served as the surgeon general of the United States under both presidents Obama and Biden, he made addressing the opioid crisis in America the focus of his tenures. As part of his national campaign, he traveled around the country to meet the families who were affected. He noticed that many expressed similar feelings of loss: "Loneliness ran like a dark thread through many of the more obvious issues that people brought to my attention, like addiction, violence, anxiety and depression," he says. As he dug in to learn more, he concluded that loneliness is the flip side of connection, and wrote his *New York Times*–bestselling book, *Together: The Healing Power of Social Connection in a Sometimes Lonely World*. In it, Dr. Murthy concludes that our need for connection is not only innate; it's evolutionary. "We're wired to associate belonging with the sharing of stories, feelings, memories, and concerns," he writes. "That's why our bodies relax and our spirits lift when we connect in genuine friendship and love." No wonder the memory of my night in Avignon has endured.

It turns out that our susceptibility to loneliness varies over our lives, ebbing and flowing as we age. Our most lonely times tend to occur when we're young and then again when we're old. What's interesting, however, is that the *way* we measure loneliness— defined as "perceived social isolation"—changes over time. In an extensive survey of over 15,000 people by Oslo University Hospital, researchers found that for younger folks (ages 18 to 29), *quantity* of relationships seemed to be the most important aspect of loneliness or connection: those who had few friends or who saw friends infrequently tended to be lonelier. But for adults who were older (ages 30–64), the *quality* of their relationships was more important: they were lonelier if they had no confidants, or people with whom they could speak intimately. Quantity of time or people wasn't as crucial. Interestingly, for the oldest group in the study (ages 65 to 79), loneliness didn't depend on how often they saw friends or whether they had someone in whom they could confide their most intimate thoughts. For them, simply having a few companionable friends or the occasional visit provided contentment enough.

Regardless of age, however, the issue of loneliness is not one to be trivialized. Dr. Murthy argues that loneliness has been associated with coronary heart disease, high blood pressure, stroke, dementia, depression, and anxiety. In other words, social bonds not only enhance how content we feel in our lives, but have significant impacts on our health, as well.

Dr. Brené Brown agrees. Brené is a research professor and the author of six *New York Times*–bestselling books on courage, vulnerability, shame, and resilience. I've known Brené for over a decade, and in watching her share her research on how to navigate the world, I notice she invariably comes back to how we are all interconnected. "Connection is why we're here," she says. "We are hardwired to connect with others, it's what gives purpose and meaning to our lives, and without it there is suffering."

But when it comes to connecting with others, Brené makes a distinction between "fitting in" and "belonging." In her research, she has found that belonging is far more desirable. "True belonging is the spiritual practice of believing in and belonging to yourself so deeply that you can share your most authentic self with the world and find sacredness in both being a part of something and standing alone in the wilderness," she writes. "True belonging doesn't require you to *change* who you are; it requires you to *be* who you are."

It had been some time since Brené wrote those words, and I was interested in learning whether her views had changed over the years. So I reached out to her. "How have your thoughts on connection and belonging evolved as you've gotten older?" I asked her.

"Well, it's complicated," she said. "Over the past twenty years, new data have reshaped some of the definitions and propositions of my work. Still, what's interesting is that the research on connection and belonging has stood both the tests of time and new data."

"How about personally?" I probed. "How has your research played out in your own life? Has your experience of your connection and belonging changed over time?"

"Oh, for sure," she said. "I think every season of our lives presents different challenges when it comes to cultivating connection and practicing belonging. Like many people, my thirties were very much about proving, performing, pleasing, and pretending. As I tried to navigate my marriage, being a new parent, and building my career, I spent way too much time worried about not being enough. The greatest gift of my forties was a unique combination of exhaustion and a really wonderful, no-bullshit therapist. I became a lot more curious about what brought me joy and connection, and a lot less interested in what other people think. I also decided that I would be the very last person I betrayed, not the first. Now, in my fifties, connection and belonging are central in my life. Before I invest time in developing relationships, before I consider saying yes to a work collaboration, or even when I'm trying to decide how to spend my time, I ask myself what the potential is for meaningful connection. I ensure it's an opportunity to be my full self."

"You know, intellectually, I fully buy into this," I said. "But I think, paradoxically, belonging isn't as tough for me as connection is. I'm a true introvert, and since the pandemic began, I fear I've become even more so. I know you're an introvert like me. So how do you make a practice of connection in a way that feels organic?"

"Well, I hate to tell you this, but connection and belonging are inextricably connected and, as a social species, we need both," she explained. "The need to belong and the need to be in meaningful connection with others is encoded in our DNA. But at this point, we know that while trying to connect and practicing belonging aren't always going to work out, it's still worth trying. We need to take the risks and make the bids with the right people."

"This sounds supremely uncomfortable," I said.

"Well, that's vulnerability for you," she responded, grinning. "Look, maintaining connection and belonging requires work. You know this. It's all about the willingness to listen, practice empathy, have hard conversations, set boundaries, ask for what we need, be other-focused. It's a commitment of showing up for each other—and of course, for great moments of laughter, joy, and shared emotion."

Studies show that people who are lonely and socially isolated are more likely to have health problems. But the converse is also true. In support of Brené's call for cultivating connection and belonging (not to mention a commitment to laughter and shared emotion), Dr. Murthy maintains that those who feel connected are more optimistic, creative, and joyful. And my dad is a shining example of this.

Every week, my father meets with a group of about eight Trinidadian friends on Zoom, to connect and, as we Trinis say, "ol' talk." Somehow, despite the fact that they've been meeting like this for over a decade, I knew nothing of this gathering until recently.

"Karen, you've never seen anything like it," my mom told me. "Sometimes I go hide in a corner and pretend I'm reading a book, but mostly I'm just eavesdropping on their conversation. They are constantly teasing each other and arguing and laughing and talking over each other." She shook her head. "For hours, the whole lot of them just get louder and louder, and all I can do is sit there and laugh."

"How do you know these people?" I asked my dad.

"Oh, some of them are friends from high school," he said. "And some of them are folks I met during my career." My dad had worked as a petroleum engineer. Given the importance of the energy industry to the Trinidadian economy, he had become well known in the country as a result.

"Is everyone in the group in oil and gas?" I asked.

"No. One is a psychiatrist. One is a doctor, and one is a dentist. There's an economist. All had very successful careers but are now retired and have been for decades. We used to meet in person at a clubhouse called the Cosmos Club in Port-of-Spain at about four-thirty in the afternoon every Friday. We'd sit at the bar, and one person would bring some street food in. I would join them every time I was back home in Trinidad, about four times a year. But then when COVID hit and Trinidad went into lockdown, the club closed. So we began meeting on Zoom."

"What do you guys talk about?"

"Well, it's just a lime!" "Lime" is a Trinidadian word we use to mean a "gathering," but with a special emphasis on connecting with each other. "And you know what happens in a lime," my dad continued. "Usually there's food and drinks, and ol' talk. And ol' talk in Trinidad is always about a subject or two or three, often going on concurrently."

"Wait . . . when you guys meet, you drink?"

Dad laughed. "Well, ah mean," he began coyly, slipping into Trinidadian pidgin. "We does all have ah *glass*! But I ent askin' what folks does have in dey glass, dat would be inappropriate!"

I laughed as well. "Okay, so what topics do you talk about when you're all together limin'?"

"We talk about topical subjects in Trinidad or the world. And even though we joke and laugh, we do address serious issues. Because of the diversity of the group, someone always has an interesting perspective that the rest of us haven't considered before. Usually, after our time together, we'll send each other articles to further expand on the issues. And then the next Friday, we'll take up the topics again or talk about new ones."

"That sounds like a *true* Trini lime." I grinned. "But this has been going on for a long time! What is it about this group that compels you to return again and again every week, for over a decade?"

Dad thought for a second. "Well, a cynic might say we're a bunch of old so-and-sos who have nothing better to do. But our love of our country keeps us going. And honestly, our friendship keeps us going."

"Say more," I urged him. "I mean, you have lots of friends. Why this particular group?"

Dad smiled. "Well, there's an old philosophical saying that when you have a friend, if your relationship ends, that friend takes a part of you with them. I think the inverse of that is also true. I think when you keep contact with your friends, they share some of themselves with you. Because of this, there's a part of you that grows. I think the word 'friendship' is about more than just being acquainted with a person. It's about someone who has touched your soul and whose soul you have touched. And I think that means that they are custodians of a part of you, and you are a custodian of a part of them. This is the way we each develop and become who we are and who we're meant to be. These friends continue to help me grow and evolve."

My dad's relationships with his friends are enviable: having connections rooted in memory and shared history is a gift. It's one that I don't share, ironically, since my father's career meant we moved frequently when I was a kid. Very few of my childhood friendships lasted longer than a year or two. So given how important connection and belonging are to our well-being, especially as we age, how do I—and others like me, who have moved around a lot in their childhoods—cultivate bonding friendships and relationships?

According to Dr. Murthy, four key strategies can help us strengthen our social connections. First, we should devote at least fifteen minutes each day to connecting with someone we care about. Second, when we do, we should fully focus on each other, eliminating distractions as we interact. Third, we should embrace solitude: according to Dr. Murthy, the first step to building stronger connections with others is to build a stronger connection with ourselves. And finally, we should develop a practice of service: doing something that taps into our gifts to help our communities, or in service of a meaningful cause. In doing so, we experience a form of human connection that reminds of us of our value and purpose. Creating habits around these four strategies not only enables us to heal our own social worlds; it creates rituals that help us thrive as we get older.

While I may not have the wealth of lifetime friendships that my dad has, I realized in reviewing these strategies that I had already begun to apply at least two of them to my life. I was getting better at my morning meditation and intention-setting, so solitude was becoming a form of daily comfort. Further, thanks to my daily habit of asking myself how I can feel more purposeful, I was always looking for ways of being in service. But the first two strategies—devoting daily focus to the people I love, and doing so without distraction—seemed more challenging.

Focusing fifteen minutes on my partner, Marcus, would be easy and a joy. But doing so with my daughter Alex would be more difficult, especially since I suspect she wouldn't love getting a phone call from her dear old mum for fifteen minutes every day while at university. Sure, I could call close friends, but my circle is small and intimate, and my friends know that I'm a confirmed introvert. They would probably begin to wonder if I was dying if I called them too many times. How could I create a practice around connecting with and appreciating the folks who mean a lot to me? And what would it look like to reconnect with those who have been important to me in the past?

Enter my friend Nancy Davis Kho. Nancy is a writer and former host of the podcast *Midlife Mixtape*, where she spoke with guests about thriving in the years "between being hip and breaking one." (Nancy wins for my friend with the wryest sense of humor.) Nancy describes the podcast and related blog as a celebration of midlife with humor, heart, and a really good beat; a "tracklist of life as a GenXer at the midpoint: blending the demands of parenting, marriage, work, and nostalgia."

She's also a writer whose work has appeared in the *Washington Post* and the *San Francisco Chronicle*, and the author of *The Thank-You Project: Cultivating Happiness*

*One Letter of Gratitude at a Time.* This book recounts her fifteen-month project of writing a series of thank-you letters to the formative people she'd encountered on the way to her fiftieth birthday. It's by turns funny and wholehearted, and I found that when I read her book, I was torn between desperately wanting to both attempt a similar project and avoid the vulnerability of ever doing so. I took my conflicted feelings as a sign that I needed to ask her more about her experience, so I contacted her.

"Tell me what prompted you to start writing these letters," I began.

"Well, when I turned fifty, my life was going really well, and I knew that I wanted to mark the year as important. I thought it would be appropriate to acknowledge people who helped, shaped, or inspired me to get to that happy point in my life. I set the goal of writing fifty letters for my fiftieth year, and it took me a little more than eighteen months to complete.

"I had written my letters to my dad and mom first, and when my dad received his, he framed it and hung it over his desk. Six months into my letter writing, my dad was diagnosed with cancer, and he died six weeks after that. Suddenly, everything in my life had changed. But when he died, it was unbelievably helpful to know that he had seen what he had meant to me and our family."

After her father's funeral, when all the activity around laying him to rest had passed, Nancy told me that writing the gratitude letters had brought comfort and inspiration in a year that had suddenly become very difficult. "Every time I wrote a letter, I would feel happier, and calmer and more peaceful," she told me. "By the time I'd written my last letter a year later, many folks knew about my project and had developed a curiosity about my letters. They asked things like how

I wrote them, and how I picked the folks who would receive them. What resulted was the book, which isn't a collection of my fifty letters, but more of a guide to writing your own letters. And when I wrote it, I made sure to include the brain science behind why doing so feels so good."

"So, why *does* it work?" I asked.

"Everyone is born with both negative recall bias and positive recall bias," she explained. Negative recall bias is beneficial, because it keeps you on alert for danger; it's what impels you to put your seatbelt on in your car, or wear a mask to avoid COVID infection. "The problem arises when you get stuck in negative recall bias, causing you to look for risk all the time," Nancy told me. "So researchers have found that an effective way to mitigate constantly living in negative recall bias is to train yourself to also tap into your *positive* recall bias. Writing these letters was a great way to do that."

"Makes sense," I said, "but fifty letters is a *lot*. How did you tackle this project?"

"I committed to writing a letter every Friday afternoon. I would actually schedule it on my calendar. It was a nice way to round out the work week: I would spend seven days thinking about the person I'd be writing to on Friday, and what I wanted to say. I tried to be very specific: thinking of what lessons they taught me, or a problem they helped me with, or the joy they brought to my life. Then Friday afternoon, I'd sit down and type a one-page, single-spaced letter to them."

Nancy found that spending an entire week thinking about kind things that people had done for her began to reframe her entire outlook. "It occurred to me that all these good feelings didn't come from the *response* to what I'd written, but the process itself," she said. "I mean, the response felt great, of course—I loved it when my dad framed his letter—but my joy was in the *writing*."

That Nancy experienced an emotional boost in writing her letters isn't surprising: research from the Greater Good Science Center at the University of California, Berkeley indicates that expressing gratitude can make people happier, improve relationships, and even counteract depression and suicidal thoughts. Moreover, it turns out that expressing gratitude might even be good for your physical health: studies indicate that people who are more grateful sleep better, have better heart health and reduced stress. It seemed that by embarking on her letter-writing project, Nancy had stumbled onto a practice that was not only lovely for the recipients of her notes but beneficial to her own health and well-being as well.

Writing gratitude letters to people who had been kind to her soon led Nancy to wonder: Would she get a similar boost in mood from writing to folks who had provided *negative* input in her life, too—the bad boyfriend, the lousy boss? Would it feel good to reframe those experiences as growth opportunities, as well? To find out, she wrote letters of gratitude to people with whom she'd had challenging relationships. "Even though I didn't send them, I found that I still got a boost from expressing my thanks for what I'd learned from those relationships," she reflected. "After that, I kept going: I wrote letters to people who weren't challenging but who weren't exactly friends, either. These were folks who were consistently kind to me—like my favorite barista, for example. I wrote to people who I saw frequently, and who went above and beyond to be generous. And I realized that I could still tap into gratitude and connection by writing them, too."

I thought back to the many people who helped our family during Hurricane Harvey: people I didn't know. Sometimes I didn't even catch their name. I mused out loud that if I were to do a thank-you project like this, I could write letters to them as well, even if I had no legitimate way to send them. "I know there are folks who helped us to whom I'll always be grateful," I said. "In fact, I always tell people that while I wouldn't wish a flood on anybody, I do wish everyone could receive the gift of being loved and cared for like we experienced during that time."

Nancy nodded. "*Exactly*. And this is the thing, right? We all have these gifts in portions, large and small, if we stop to look for them. That's what my gratitude letter project does: it gives you a framework to stop and say, 'Okay, College Roommate, maybe it seemed pretty small at the time that you helped tutor me in calculus, but that was the class I needed to graduate on time, and because of you I did, which led to these other cool things.' And honestly, one of the gifts of aging is that you get *perspective*. You're able to see why these kindnesses were so impactful in your life. And writing these letters hooks into that perspective, and helps build those feelings of connection and gratitude."

Nancy had almost convinced me to write thank-you letters as part of my bid to increase and deepen connections in my life. Almost. But the idea of writing such letters struck me as incredibly vulnerable, in a way I didn't love. "I think if I wrote letters to some of these folks, it would feel awkward—especially sending letters to people I haven't seen in a long time," I told her. "And wouldn't the people who I see every day feel really weird, suddenly receiving this formal, physical letter from me? How did you get over that vulnerability?"

"Well, researchers have found that people tend to overestimate how awkward it will feel to send the letter, and underestimate how happy the recipient will be to receive it," Nancy said. "So part of getting over that feeling of vulnerability is knowing that you're probably making it bigger in your mind than it really is. But the other thing to remember is that writing these letters is *of benefit to the writer*. While writing these letters does provide the added benefit of making someone else happier, you never have to send the letters. There's no Thank-You Note Police."

After our conversation, I pulled out my copy of *The Thank-You Project* as I mulled over what she said. I wasn't sure that I had it in me to write as many as fifty letters, but I figured at the very least, I could write thank-you letters to my parents. My parents are both in their eighties, and it was definitely time for me to let them know how much I appreciated them. I opened my laptop and, using Nancy's book as a guide, I began each letter the same way:

*Dear Mom/Dad:*

*As you know, this year I turn 55 years old. I've had such a fortunate life that I decided the best way to commemorate this Emerald Jubilee year (who knew that's what it's called?) is to write thank-you letters to the people who have enriched my life along the way. Today, you and Mom/Dad drew the short straw—you both had to be the first people to get these letters, for obvious reasons.*

In each of their letters, I wrote about the lessons I remember them teaching me when I was a child. But I also wrote about the moments we shared that were so special to me that I tried to replicate them for my daughter when I became a parent. I wrote about how they've helped me even as an adult.

As I wrote each letter, I surprised myself by how easily I was able to coax memories to the surface: ones which I hadn't thought of in decades but that had clearly helped form my worldview. If you'd asked me before I'd written these letters, I would have told you that my mother was primarily the nurturer and my father the teacher of how to navigate the world. But as I wrote, I realized how many additional lessons about engaging with the different cultures of the world came from my mother, and how many caring moments came from my dad.

As I sealed each letter, I experienced that pang of gratitude, calm, and well-being that Nancy promised I would feel. *Huh,* I thought. *Maybe I* could *write a few dozen letters after all.*

The next time Marcus, Alex, and I had lunch with my parents, I handed them their envelopes as we said goodbye. "What's this?" my dad asked, turning his envelope over in his hand.

"Just something for you both," I replied. "It's not money."

"Oh," said my dad, grinning. "Well, I guess I'll take it anyway."

Later, each of my parents called me: First, my mom, who tearfully thanked me for my words. Then my dad, asking if it was okay to frame my letter and put it above his desk. I laughed, thinking about Nancy's dad who did the same. And I was suddenly overwhelmed with relief that I wrote these notes to them while they are still with us.

I committed to writing more thank-you notes, setting the goal of fifty-five letters during my fifty-fifth year—but also promising that I'd give myself some grace if it didn't happen. Taking Nancy's advice, I typed each of these letters, saving them in a single document on my computer, and simply printing the appropriate pages when it came time to send them. Each time I wrote a note—to my best friends, an old professor long-since passed, the emergency room team at the local hospital in 1997 (long story)—I felt a pang of gratitude. But more importantly, I reinvigorated the connection I felt to each of these people. Each letter served as a reminder that we all have the capacity to leave a mark on each other's lives, often in ways that we don't necessarily expect.

I thought about human connection a lot that summer, as we spent most of our energy preparing for our only child to leave for university. A few weeks before I'd spoken to Nancy, Alex had graduated from a school she'd attended since she was seven years old. It's a tiny Montessori school near our home, a school that produced a close-knit graduating class of only twenty-one students. In the months after graduation, Alex and her classmates had been inseparable: they all hung out at each other's houses, visited the fast-food restaurants where several had summer jobs, and took day trips together. They were very aware that their time together was limited, and that, come September, they would be thousands of miles apart. At her young age, Alex had already developed the kinds of relationships that prompted Nancy, and now me, to embark on our letter-writing projects. She had already met people who were helping, shaping, and influencing her to become the person she is meant to be. And at eighteen years old, she still had so many more of those kinds of folks to meet.

That summer was an exhilarating, if disorienting, time. It was clear that Alex was happy, and we were happy for her. Watching her place treasured belongings in shipping boxes, as she animatedly spoke about what she hoped her new city would be like, was heartening. Yet I had to admit I was feeling another, underlying feeling. Not *sadness*, exactly, but something different. When I tried to describe the emotion my friend Asha, who had already experienced dropping two kids off at college, she understood immediately. "Yup, I remember that feeling with my son," she said. "It was like suddenly a roller-coaster operator was buckling my seatbelt, it was about to lurch forward. All I wanted to yell was, 'Wait. WAIT. I *have* to go on this ride, don't I?!'"

Exactly. I was thrilled for Alex, as things were unfolding exactly as she'd hoped. But as excited as we were for her, I couldn't help but panic a little, wondering if there were any Great Insights or Life Lessons that we'd failed to impart before she left to live on her own. But the roller coaster was leaving the platform.

The time finally came. We landed in Chicago on a late August night, checked into our Airbnb, and passed out, knowing our extensive to-do list required an early alarm. The next few days were filled with trips to big-box stores, buying all the items that it hadn't made sense to ship ahead: a side table for her dorm room bed, a couple of lamps, extension cables, shower caddies. By the time we arrived at her residence hall, we had three huge rolling suitcases and scores of giant shopping bags. When we entered her room, I was surprised that it was brighter, airier, and bigger than we had anticipated. The boxes we'd shipped were on one side of the room, her roommate's were on another.

Her roommate wasn't scheduled to arrive for a couple of days, so Alex quickly picked her side of the room, and Marcus began helping her unpack while I made her bed. The strange roller-coaster feeling began to subside and was replaced with enthusiasm. Alex's excitement was infectious. Her eyes danced as she directed us where to hang string lights and posters. We watched it dawn on her that this was *her* domain now; her parents' opinions about how to create a comfortable space took a back seat to her own. After a few hours of hard work, she'd created a cheery oasis, and the three of us rewarded ourselves with a large Chicago-style deep-dish.

"What do you think?" I whispered to Marcus when she wasn't paying attention.

"Oh, she's gonna be *fine*," he responded through a mouthful of pizza. I tried to think of a reason to protest, but I couldn't. She did, indeed, seem ready.

Alex spent the next couple of nights in her dorm room alone, but every morning we met her for breakfast and then spent the days sightseeing in her new town: Shedd Aquarium, the architectural boat tour on the Chicago River, Navy Pier. After a few days, Alex had a decent understanding of the layout of her section of the city. And after repeatedly witnessing the check-in process of the students by the residence hall as she came and went, Marcus and I were comfortable that her university took the safety of the students seriously.

The night before her roommate was scheduled to move in, Alex spent the night with us in our Airbnb. She figured that Maria would want to unpack with her parents in solitude. The girls had already struck up a warm camaraderie: they had met over social media, and from their respective homes in Texas and Kansas, they'd spent the summer sharing Pinterest boards and Amazon wish lists, coordinating what they wanted their new dorm room to look like. We headed over to the residence hall at around midday, and when the girls finally laid eyes on each other, they shrieked with excitement, hugging each other like old friends. I looked around: Maria and her parents had clearly worked hard that morning. Save for a few items to hang on the wall, the room décor was complete. It was bright and cozy and exactly what you would hope your kid's home for the next nine months would look like.

Maria's mom approached me. "This place is pretty great," she said.

"For sure," I grinned. "I don't remember my grubby dorm looking this good when I was in college."

"Think if we moved in with them, they'd notice?" she said, her eyes twinkling.

"I should think they'd be grateful to have us," I said. "Do you want to break the news to them that we're not leaving, or should I?"

I knew I was going to miss Alex tremendously, but it was a huge comfort to know that she was excited about university, she already loved her roommate, and she would be living in a comfortable, safe space. It was hard to feel sad when this is what we'd hoped for her: to attend a university she loved, to study something she's passionate about, with people she liked was always the goal. Besides, what adventures lay ahead for these two young women? Could Maria be one of the people who will influence Alex in a way for which she'll feel immense gratitude for the rest of her life?

As everyone turned to walk out, I closed my eyes and silently prayed that this would be the case. Then I opened my day bag and pulled out a thank-you note I had written before we left Houston, and I tucked it under my daughter's pillow.

# PART IV

# Envision

# EIGHT

# Mission Possible

There's a great story about Alfred Nobel, a Swedish chemist whose claim to fame was as an inventor, most notably of dynamite. A savvy businessman, he amassed a fortune in the commercialization of instruments of war, owning nearly one hundred factories that made explosives and munitions.

In 1888 when Nobel was fifty-five years old, his brother Ludvig died of cardiac arrest in Cannes, France. The newspapers reported the death but mistook Ludvig for Alfred, with one paper proclaiming, "Le marchand de la mort est mort!" ("the merchant of death is dead!"). What followed was a scathing obituary, describing how Alfred had grown wealthy developing new ways to "mutilate and kill."

While the newspaper later issued a correction, it wasn't quick enough. Alfred had read the words, and legend has it that he was deeply unsettled by the premature obituary in which his apparently negative global reputation had been laid bare. It's for this reason, it is said, that a year before his death in 1896, the never-married Alfred secretly signed his last will and testament, leaving his considerable wealth (about $265 million in today's dollars) for the establishment of a series of prizes for "those who, during the preceding year, shall have conferred the greatest benefit on mankind." Most notable was the establishment of the fifth Nobel award, designated for "the person who shall have done the most or the best work for fraternity between the nations and the abolition or reduction of standing armies and the formation and spreading of peace congresses."

Now: This story might be apocryphal, as there's no telling whether the false obituary was the true catalyst behind Nobel's bequest. But I do love the idea that if it weren't for the false obituary prompting Alfred to clarify his mission, we might not have the Nobel Peace Prize today. In any event, the lesson is this: While most of us won't have the experience of reading our own obituary while we're still alive (and hopefully we won't be known as the "merchant of death," either), as we grow older, we always have the opportunity to clarify and then reclarify our life's purpose, just like Alfred Nobel. And the surprisingly good news is that reclarification of life's meaning has health and longevity benefits, too.

Purposeful living has been linked to all sorts of traits of well-being, including lower risk of disease, better sleep, and healthier behaviors. Dr. Patrick Hill, associate professor of psychological and brain sciences at Washington University in St. Louis and its Purpose, Aging, Transitions and Health (PATH) Lab, has found a direct connection between purpose in life and cognitive functioning in adulthood. His team's research indicates that purpose in life is associated with "higher scores for memory, executive functioning and overall cognition" as we get older. Furthermore, a greater sense of purpose has been found to decrease risk of degenerative and age-associated disorders like stroke, myocardial infarction, and disability. And if that's not enough, identifying a purpose for your life may, in fact, add years to it.

In other words, living purposefully is key to living well and perhaps living *longer*. It's no wonder, then, that as we approach the central portion of our lives, clarifying our callings becomes more important to us.

※

After I spent two years at St. Joseph's Convent and right before my sixteenth birthday, my father earned another promotion that required relocating back to Houston, Texas. At the time, I'd just finished my Ordinary Levels exams, earned my General Certificate of Education, and was slated to continue my schooling at Convent for two more years to pursue my Advanced Levels exams. This move, which was unexpected, would scuttle those plans. Within weeks of hearing the news, we packed up our house and headed back to America. My parents found a home in the suburbs of Houston, and once we'd settled in, they enrolled me in Cy-Fair High School as a sixteen-year-old senior. This would give me a year to reacclimate to the United States while I applied to university.

My father had big dreams that I would follow in his engineering footsteps, so even though I'd focused on foreign languages for my O-Levels, I spent my senior year at Cy-Fair taking primarily science and mathematics courses: physics, chemistry, calculus. I was hoping to leave the state for college and applied to several universities on the East and West Coasts. But when Texas A&M University offered me a full scholarship, there was simply no denying the relief on my dad's face as he stared at the letter. Even though the thought of going to school in a city like Los Angeles or Philadelphia had captured my imagination, I had made some friends at my new high school who were also planning to go to A&M; suddenly, the idea of going somewhere where I knew folks became surprisingly comforting.

So off I went to College Station to major in civil engineering, to the delight of my parents. Their approval was addictive: it was at Texas A&M where I began an extended period of following everyone's guidance—or what I assumed would be their guidance—except my own. But after I graduated and worked for a year as an engineer, I finally figured out that engineering really wasn't my thing.

I considered my options. Becoming an attorney seemed to me the only acceptable alternative to being an engineer (not that my parents or anyone else in my life had ever actually voiced this). So I applied to law school. I earned my law degree while working full-time, taking as many intellectual property law classes as I could. After all, everyone who knew that I had an engineering degree told me that IP law was the proper career path for "someone like me." Following graduation, I got various jobs in a couple of Fortune 500 companies as an in-house software licensing attorney. After all, professors and mentors insisted those were "ideal" jobs for a person with my educational background. Eventually, I was named chief counsel of a subsidiary of a global energy services company, then chief of staff of the parent corporation. After all, those were the "obvious" next steps for my career.

And then I did the most irrational, un-rule-following thing I had ever done in my life.

I quit.

After fourteen years of practicing law, I decided to stop. By then I was working long hours, married and parenting a little girl. I was exhausted, and I was burnt out. So for the first time in my life, I left a job without another position waiting for me. I had no discernible plan. All I knew was that with a five-year-old at home, if I was going to work long hours to exhaustion, I was going to do work that I loved rather than work that was expected of me.

Once I was no longer waking up to go to an office, I decided to lean into the sorts of activities I loved to do when I wasn't working. Writing, photography, speaking: these were the activities that brought me an inordinate amount of joy. I already had a years-old daily writing and photography practice that I published in blog form, and I had spoken at several conferences about the benefits of doing so. I announced to whomever would listen that I was available to do any and all of those things for pay. Slowly, opportunities to do combinations of those activities began appearing. I traveled to Africa as a photojournalist, and I was hired to speak at various workshops and organizations. I wrote and contributed to books on creativity and self-exploration. And with each opportunity, I learned more about the activities that brought meaning to my own life. I discovered that filling my life with purposeful work was, in fact, possible.

While I'd love to believe that getting curious about the activities that fueled my soul was uniquely insightful, it turns out I'm not particularly special. The need for meaning and purpose in our lives is a motivation intrinsic to us all. Viktor Frankl, the author of *Man's Search for Meaning*, was a Jewish psychologist imprisoned at Auschwitz. While there, he offered his services as a therapist to his fellow prisoners. Upon his release, Frankl, inspired by what he witnessed of his compatriots during his time in the brutal camp, wrote his book in nine days. "There is nothing in the world, I venture to say," he declared, "that would so effectively help one to survive even the worst conditions as the knowledge that there is meaning in one's life." He further insisted that being human "always points, and is directed, to something or someone other than oneself. The more one forgets himself—by giving himself to a cause to serve or another person to love—the more human he is and the more he actualizes himself." In other words, the urge to be of service is one of our most distinguishing design features.

Three years after I stopped practicing law, while I wasn't making the kind of money I had as the chief counsel of a software company, I was doing work I fully believed in. My work lit me up: I was excited to get up every day, be creative, and produce offerings that brought joy or clarity to others. I was still in full experimental mode, trying opportunities that sounded fun and interesting, to see if I might like doing more of them. If you had asked me why they brought meaning to my life, I'm not sure I could have articulated it. I just knew they did.

Around this time, my friend Erin Loechner published what she called "a personal mission statement" for her life and career on her blog: "I will encourage the discouraged. I will befriend the friendless, include the excluded and feed the creatively starved. I refuse to take life too seriously. At the same time, I will honor its weight. I will respect the time I am given. I will live a purposeful life. I will support. I will smile at strangers. I will smile at myself."

Her personal mission statement was short and sweet. But it was clear how such a statement could be a tool of discernment, helping her navigate opportunities as they arose, acting as a north star. Inspired, I tried my hand at writing my own, in an attempt to codify my own thoughts of what I wanted my life and my work to stand for. I called it a *spark statement*, because this was the spark from which the meaning of my work—and frankly, my life—was born. It read as follows:

I believe in the interconnectedness of all who
inhabit our planet.

I engage in the relentless pursuit of real,
uncontrived beauty, in every form.

I illustrate that beauty is everywhere, even
(and sometimes especially) in the most
unlikely places.

In so doing, I work tirelessly to counter
negativity, violence, discrimination, and
desperation,

and join forces with those who celebrate
positivity, peace, kindness, and joy.

I convince the skeptical of their uncommon
beauty,

and I create tools to help the weary see the
inherent power they hold in their own
lives.

I provide hard, irrefutable evidence that
there is good in the world,

and I am fiercely dedicated to showing how
beautiful our planet really is,

one image at a time.

I published it on my site, and over the years it became the lens through which I made all the major decisions of my life, both personal and professional. Simply expressing what I want to stand for was instrumental in curating and attracting joy.

My friend Brad Montague once told me everyone should have a spark statement, or something like it. Brad is an artist, illustrator, and the *New York Times*–bestselling author of *Becoming Better Grownups,* a whimsical primer for adults about how to find purpose and meaning. Brad proudly admits to having a manifesto, but he also tells me that every once in a while, he revisits it. "I add to it or even rewrite it, as a prayer to help me get greater clarity on what it is I believe, what I want, what is lacking in my life or in my relationships, or what I want to add to it," he told me.

Sometimes, he says, he looks at old things he's written and thinks, *Where did that guy go? What happened to him?* "I still believe in the work in my bones, but it's like I've gotten beaten up or beaten down, and I'll have forgotten its importance to me," he said. For other things he's written or said or done, however, he thinks, "Oh I wouldn't do or say that now." "As I've grown, it's a dance of hanging on to the things that I need to and forgetting the things I need to unlearn," he said. "And I really think there's something to keeping that part of you engaged: that thing that makes you most alive, the soul of your work, and that must be tended to."

I wrote my spark statement eleven years ago. And while I still believed in its words, perhaps it was time to take Brad's advice and reexamine or even rewrite it. After all, much has changed in eleven years—hell, *I've* changed in eleven years. Did those words still represent what means the most to me? Did it still encompass everything I want my work and life to stand for? Or would I need to scratch everything and start over?

I assumed that, over the years, I'd collected some experience, skills, and an expanded worldview that could help frame my purpose. Surely, by midlife, we all have. So as I asked myself these questions, I wondered if my friends had experienced a similar reckoning. Unsurprisingly, they had.

Take, for example, Linda Lorelle. Linda is an Emmy-award-winning journalist and communications professional who anchored the evening news for almost seventeen years at Houston's NBC affiliate, KPRC-TV. A native of Chicago, Linda has led a twisty-turny life full of adventure, as she followed her curiosity to actualizing her life's mission. And it all started, as many good journeys do, with dance.

"I started dancing when I was four years old," Linda told me. "I danced throughout my childhood and all through college, as I was getting my undergraduate degree. While I was a student, I would drive to Oakland from Palo Alto to take dance classes. To this day, I still dance. In fact, I have a dance class tomorrow. Dancing is my spiritual practice. It feeds my soul."

Linda has a developmental psychology degree, with a secondary degree in Italian, from Stanford University. As a student, she thought she would one day open a school for underserved kids to get a stellar preschool education, one that would set them up for success later in life. But after graduation, she decided the first thing she wanted to do was pursue dance professionally. She figured if professional dance didn't work out, she had a degree that would allow her to pursue something else. She ended up dancing in Chicago and New York City.

Then one day in class, she went to do a jump and her muscle twisted and snapped. "And that was it," she told me. "It ended my dance career in an instant."

"Oh no!" I said. "So what did you do? Did you begin teaching, working with kids?"

"Actually, no. When I was recovering from my injury and unable to dance, I remembered a friend who worked in television news, who had once said that whenever I was ready to hang up my dance shoes for whatever reason, I should consider a job in television. I was intrigued, especially since I'd always considered myself as a communicator. Even when I was a little kid, I pictured myself as a mediator, trying to bring two sides together. So on a whim, I decided to enroll in a broadcasting trade school."

At that time, Linda was waitressing at an Italian restaurant on the Upper West Side of Manhattan, a job that she was able to get because she spoke Italian. It also happened to be a favorite hangout of the news team of the show *60 Minutes*. "One night, I was chatting to them because they were sitting at one of my tables, and they asked me about my story. So I told them," she said. "One of the guys who was there was a producer, and unexpectedly, he offered to introduce me to the director of minority recruitment for CBS. Because of that introduction and the subsequent meeting, where the director gave me a generous amount of his time and feedback, I decided to go back to school for my master's degree in journalism."

"Wow. That's some pretty serendipitous stuff," I said. She nodded. "So you get your master's degree, have this amazing career as a broadcast journalist for *years*, and even win an Emmy! Good decision, then?"

"*Great* decision."

"But you eventually left television and are now a communications consultant. Is this what living your life's purpose looks like?"

"Well, it's definitely me living my *passion*," she clarified. "My passion is storytelling. That's different from my *mission*."

"How?"

"Well, storytelling is what I love to do: it's what broadcast journalism allowed me to do, and it's what I do now, as a communications professional. But my purpose is connection, and my mission is to add more love and light in the world. By doing well in pursuing my passion, I'm able to fulfill my purpose and my mission."

"Oh, this is such an important distinction," I said. "And this, I assume, is where the Linda Lorelle

Scholarship Fund comes in?" Linda's scholarship fund offers college scholarships, support, and guidance to Houston-area students in need of financial assistance. Working with school districts in and around the Houston area, the fund invites high school juniors to apply for the scholarship, and then awards the scholarships at the beginning of their senior year. Students agree to attend seminars about how to be successful during post-high school education and life: résumé-writing, filling out college and financial aid applications, and interviewing.

"Exactly. My mother used to always say to me, 'Linda, when you've given of yourself, you've given the most,'" Linda said. "I grew up watching my parents give back to our community in Chicago, and remember, when I was at Stanford, I'd considered starting a school. So when I was promoted from weekend to primetime anchor, I knew it was time to do something with all this visibility that I suddenly had. My husband, Lou, and I had moved to Houston so I could anchor at KPRC-TV, so I wanted to do something for this community that had embraced us so fully."

Lou and Linda are both passionate about education, and they wanted to do something to help kids go to college. "But we didn't want to help the students in the top 5 or 10 percent of their class, because there are already lots of resources that help top performers," she told me. "We were more interested in the kids who were middle-of-the-road: the ones who might have average grades because of the circumstances they were born into over which they have no control. The kids who might have parents who struggle with addiction or are in prison. The kids who aren't able to focus 100 percent of their time and ability on school because they're dealing with *life*. The priorities they must make around their schooling because of challenges they face: these aren't an indication of their intelligence or capability or motivation to make something of their lives." Students who have received the scholarship have gone on to become executives, teachers, school principals, and one is even the executive producer of a national news program.

I asked Linda what she was envisioning for herself as she thinks about her mission, legacy, and purpose. Had it changed since she and her husband started the scholarship fund? Linda didn't even hesitate in her answer. "I'm *really* focused on doing whatever I can to help strengthen and save our democracy," she said. "The Linda Lorelle Scholarship Fund is certainly a part of that, because I think investing in the education of future generations always helps. But also, I'll continue to bring us all together as humans through storytelling. I'll use my podcast as a tool for sharing connecting conversations—whatever it takes. I'm very clear on my purpose, and I intend to keep using my passions to realize it."

Linda's grounded confidence in her life's purpose was earned over a lifetime of continually clarifying her values, following her curiosity, and internalizing the lessons that she learned on the way. While she began her adulthood believing that she was destined to start a school, over time she discovered that her desire to help kids access strong educational opportunities involved her using her gifts in a different, creative way. Her experience is a great example of how sometimes fully understanding your personal mission involves not just curiosity but experience.

Mira Jacob is equally clear on her calling, also largely formed by her life's path. She's a novelist, memoirist, and cultural critic. Her book *The Sleepwalker's Guide to Dancing* was named a best book of the year by *Time*, *Esquire*, *Publisher's Weekly*, and *Library Journal*. Her graphic memoir, *Good Talk: A Memoir in Conversations*, was shortlisted for the National Book Critics Circle award, longlisted for the PEN Open Book Award, and named a *New York Times* Notable Book. Mira is also a visiting professor at The New School in New York City, as well as a founding faculty member of the MFA program at Randolph College.

In other words, she's impressive. What's most impressive about Mira, however, is the clarity with which she speaks of her personal mission. But that didn't come easily.

"When you first met me, Karen, I hadn't yet reconciled my activist self with my professional self," she explained. "I had my professional life, and my activism was on the side. And I still hadn't published my first novel yet. It took me a long time to break into publishing because for so many years, as an Indian American writer, I was told my stories were either too Indian or not Indian enough. The traditional way I learned to write was through workshops, where everyone tells you what they think about your work, and there's a 'right way' to do things—and let's face it, that way was usually framed through a white lens. I was told that there was no room for me as an Indian writer. That as an Indian writer, I need to explain myself. Karen, it was so awful. I spent so much time trying to be the kind of Indian they felt sure they would let in the room, as opposed to the kind of Indian that I am and was—which wasn't the right one for them."

Mira moved to New York City when she was twenty-four years old, and her mother gave her some advice. Her mother had grown up in Mumbai, India, but her parents raised her and her brother in the village of

Corrales, New Mexico. Her mother said to her, "Mira, you've never lived in a big city, and everyone has always known who you are in this town. When you move to New York, I want you to remember there's always going to be someone who is smarter, more beautiful, richer, better employed, or with better opportunities than you have; that's what living in a big city is about. Do not find your happiness by trying to be the best as compared to other people. Find your happiness from trying to be your best as compared to yourself."

"That's good advice, man," I said.

"Isn't it? So, when I wrote *The Sleepwalker's Guide to Dancing*, I ended up writing it for *me*. And it was a lot. It was a book about death. It was a book about fathers. But it was also about what it means to be in America and be the 'right Indian' versus the 'wrong Indian.' It wrestled with the way my family was welcomed in the sixties and able to buy a home and integrate in society in New Mexico—but why, when driving through the state, I would see reservations and see how the 'wrong Indian' wasn't given any of the access that we were. This concept haunts my second book, *Good Talk*, as well. But *Sleepwalker's* was when I really learned to play with the thoughts that hobbled me—just *play* with them, without trying to make sense of them or even interpret them for someone else. Of course, eventually, after ten years the book got published. And the rest is history."

"But this experience—this experience of playing with your writing, taking forever to break into publishing, trying to mold yourself into something that you could never be, your mother's advice," I asked, "did all this help formulate what you see as your life's purpose?"

"Absolutely," she said. "It plays out in my role as a professor. I'm really devoted to the idea of ensuring that my students tell their story, and I think my job is to remove obstacles to help them unlock their most intuitive play so they can do so. Many of my students are people of color, and the truth is we don't have the opportunity to play with the way we tell our stories very often. We walk into the room thinking we need to be perfect, and we walk in intent on showing everyone that we deserve to be there. But I'm interested in what happens when we allow ourselves to play: to get into those softer parts and fail a little and try things. I feel like if there is anything I'm supposed to be doing on this earth, it's to continually create the spaces where that kind of play can happen, the kinds of spaces where they can access their own power. Because I believe in that power."

Like Linda, while Mira's passions *differ* from her mission, they *support* her mission. Mira is passionate about her writing and teaching, but her mission is to create spaces where up-and-coming writers are able to play with their own art to tell their stories. And like Linda, Mira's mission isn't focused on her own success; rather, it's about taking the lessons learned from her own life experiences and using them in service of others. Mira's career as a writer led her to her mission as a teacher and mentor. Through her efforts, the rest of us have access to more diverse and innovative stories.

Tarana Burke discovered her passion for service very early on. Tarana has been working at the intersection of racial justice, arts and culture, anti-violence, and gender equity ever since she was a young girl in the 1980s. In her *New York Times*–bestselling memoir, *Unbound: My Story of Liberation and the Birth of the Me Too Movement*, she describes a time when her calling became clear. As a young woman in Selma, Alabama, she worked with dozens of young Black women who had survived violence, sexual abuse, and exploitation. "I needed to turn my focus to building a sense of self-worth in Black girls," she writes. "What I saw missing in so many of these girls was a connection to how *valuable* their lives, current and future, were. As a result, they didn't talk about the abuse or the longing for death or any of the twists and turns between those two places that made their young lives infinitely more complicated. I had spent many years feeling the same way about myself."

In the years since that time, Tarana founded the #MeToo movement, a social crusade focused on assisting a global community of survivors of sexual assault. The #MeToo movement has become an international juggernaut, and the heightened awareness of the issue of sexual harassment and abuse that the movement inspired has had real results. Nineteen states have enacted new protections for victims of sexual assault, and more than two hundred bills aimed at deterring harassment have been introduced in state legislatures.

It had been several years since 2017, when #MeToo went viral, catapulting Tarana into global prominence in the conversation around sexual violence. I wondered if the ensuing fame, combined with her previous decades of social justice work, had affected or transformed what she viewed as her personal call to action. So I reached out to her and asked if she'd spend some time with me sharing her thoughts, and she graciously agreed.

"For the entire time I've been an activist, I've always wanted to see large-scale organizing around sexual violence. I've always wanted to see people take the work of ending sexual violence as seriously as they do the work of ending gun violence, or climate change, or police violence—any of the huge social justice issues we see today. I wanted to see the same level of passion and commitment from everyday people, not just from survivors or women or people who felt intimately connected to the issue. I wanted people to see sexual violence as an injustice against humanity. And even after #MeToo went viral, we saw a lot of media amplification but not necessarily a lot of response. So I began to think that kind of focus was just fantasy—it was never going to happen. And then came the Brett Kavanaugh hearings."

In July 2018, then-president Donald Trump nominated Judge Brett Kavanaugh to the Supreme Court of the United States. During the confirmation hearings, it came to light that Christine Blasey Ford, a psychology professor and former classmate of Kavanaugh's, had written a letter to Senator Dianne Feinstein accusing Kavanaugh of sexual assault when they were both in high school in 1982. "There was this interesting moment where several women's organizations came together to determine how they could support Dr. Ford, including writing an open letter to her, and a call to action to rally in Washington, DC during the hearings," Tarana told me. She signed the letter and made plans to fly to DC for the rally.

The day of the rally arrived. It was raining, and she was sure that no one would come. "But when I arrived, thousands of people had shown up, and continued to show up for a full week of events," she remembered. Tarana took a deep breath. "That week was so pivotal for me, especially in light of everything that has happened in the last five years. I hadn't realized until that moment that I'd never dreamed *big* enough. I mean, I had imagined this movement, but it was sort of a fantasy that I had put on a shelf. I wasn't living into it. I had defaulted to what was simple and practical—which is important to do, because often progress is made in simple and practical acts. But I wasn't sustaining the larger level of hope and vision needed to make a large movement happen. It was like I'd dreamed it up and then put it on a shelf."

I knew Tarana was about to celebrate a milestone birthday herself. And I wondered: Now that she had evidence that she could dream big and manifest huge things, what was she dreaming about doing now?

Tarana's response was quick. "I think now is the time when I need to dust off old dreams," she said. "Writing has always been a big dream of mine, and after publishing my memoir, I'm looking forward to writing more. I have a production deal with a television network, so I'm working on developing content for television. I'm just interested in looking at the dreams that I've shelved in the past and how I can bring them to fruition."

And then she paused. "I think it's important to dream big, but my advice to myself, and to others too, is to not stop learning and creating. I've been doing this work for a long time, and I think when you do work for a while, you get to a point where you can do it in your sleep and become stagnant. I can hold the vision, but it's important for me to allow younger folks to bring fresh ideas to the vision while I keep learning. I think my job is to become bigger as a person—through learning and creating—so that my work can get bigger."

What's particularly interesting about the stories of these women is how their callings both evolved over time and returned them to who they are. Linda wanted to start a preschool when she was a young woman; now she enables kids to get higher education. Mira wrestled with questions of identity and cultural origin; now she helps young writers to wrestle with the same questions in a nonjudgmental space and share their stories to help the rest of us deepen our understanding of each other. And Tarana's story of continuing to interrogate what she stood for, and being unafraid to return to examine past dreams, struck a chord with me. As I thought about my own mission, encompassed by my spark statement, I realized that it didn't reflect, in any deep way, the lessons and experiences I'd gleaned from the past decade. It did not yet push me to recall former dreams of mine that I could actualize in my future.

My friend Justine is known for saying "the first half of your life is biographical, and the second half of your life is autobiographical." In other words, the experiences of the first half of your life give you the wisdom to be an active creator and architect of the second half of your life. The story of Alfred Nobel is a prime example of this sentiment, as are the lives of Linda Lorelle, Mira Jacob, and Tarana Burke.

As I considered my own life in this moment— decades of work experience behind me, my only daughter leaving home to go to university and begin creating a life of her own, and hopefully decades of life yet ahead of me—it seemed time to begin "writing my autobiography," so to speak. It was time to take stock of what I'd learned about myself—the triumphs and the lessons— and revisit my spark statement with a wider lens.

I grabbed my notebook and scrawled at the top of the first clean page: *What were the most challenging parts of the past fifty-five years?* I considered the question, and then began writing stream-of-consciousness, without a break.

I wrote about how challenging it was in my teenage years, moving back and forth between countries, having to code-switch between two very different cultures. I wrote about the challenges of entering college at seventeen years old, living with a roommate for the first time, and learning to navigate a decidedly American college experience, especially being the only Black woman student in the civil engineering department. I wrote about working in the energy industry, first as a junior structural engineer, and then attending law school at night and becoming an attorney. I wrote about marrying, divorcing, and then marrying again, after having moved alone across the Atlantic for new adventures in the United Kingdom: a new, different country from the two where I'd finally acquired some comfort. I reflected on becoming a parent, protecting our family as we took shelter from Hurricane Harvey, losing everything to its floodwaters and having to literally rebuild from the ground up . . . and retreating again, as a virulent pandemic overtook the world. I wrote about triumphs and heartbreaks and abundance and loss, until I couldn't think of anything else to write.

And then I scrawled a new question at the top of the next page: *What are the lessons that all these challenges taught me?*

This was a harder question to tackle, mostly because there were so many. My father's career that forced so many family moves, as well as my university years, taught me what it feels like to be an outsider, certainly; but the experiences also taught me empathy and curiosity. I discovered that while assimilation into a new culture feels minimizing, integration with a new culture, bringing my whole self to a new place, while learning everything I can about it, can feel *expanding*. I've discovered that I can figure out pretty much anything if I put my mind to it. I learned what partnership means, especially in my marriage, as Marcus and I raised our daughter and faced literal natural disasters and pandemics together. We are very different people, he and I, but I've learned that his preternatural calm is the perfect foil for my drive for solving urgent problems. The truth is that despite the craziness we've faced together over the years, we've grown closer than ever.

I've learned that insecurities are universal, and yet, by tapping into the best versions of ourselves, we each have the power to curate the person we'd like to become. I've learned that all over the world, the similarities we share bind us together in a global village, but the differences we bring make that village infinitely beautiful. And I've learned that my superpowers—traits I believe I've been given to use in service—include compassion, sensitivity, the ability to find and appreciate beauty, and the facility to communicate that beauty as best as possible, using both words and images.

These lessons seemed like gifts. But as with most blessings in life, I knew that putting these teachings to good use is what would make them valuable. Thus the next question presented itself: *What issues are most important to me now?*

This was easy: discrimination and bigotry were still at the top of the list of issues that get under my skin, ones that spark instant fury when I witness them. But in addition to the discrimination that we often inflict against each other, I've grown deeply interested in the discrimination that we can direct inwardly: the nagging idea that maybe if we just weren't so [insert race/age/ability/color/size/gender identity/sexual orientation-related word here], we'd be more worthy or attractive or loveable. I will always be interested in fighting external, societal bigotry, but I'm intrigued by what I can do to help people dispel their internalized discriminatory thoughts as well. Surely, with my life experience, skills, and gifts, I could be of service. I want to spend the second half of my life being open and experimental in figuring out how to make this happen.

At this point, I was almost ready to rewrite my spark statement, but I had two more questions I wanted to ask myself: *What is my vision? And what mission do I accept in response?*

I closed my eyes for a second to reflect. And then I opened my eyes and began to write.

*My vision is of a world where people create and curate their best selves, free from societal, cultural, or capitalistic expectations that prey on their feeling smaller than the radiant beings they're designed to be.* The words came surprisingly quickly. But I knew that after everyone I'd spoken to, the practices I'd experimented with, and the introspection I'd done, it was exactly what I hoped for the future. And once my vision had crystallized, my mission came easily: *to live big, free, and expansively, and to help others do the same.*

I reread everything I had scrawled in my journal. It was time to write a new spark statement. Here's what I came up with:

> *Despite the darkness, there is always light,*
> *and it exists in each of us:*
> *no matter our race or national origin (because of it),*
> *no matter our gender (because of it),*
> *no matter how we love (because of it),*
> *no matter our age (because of it).*
> *Using everything I am and have been—*
> *my culture, my talents, my education, and my*
> *    experience—*
> *I convince the skeptical of their uncommon light,*
> *illustrating the inherent power we each have to*
> *    make the world a better place.*
> *May my words and images shine bright enough to*
> *    extinguish*

*the darkness of negativity, violence, and discrimination,*
*and instead illuminate positivity, peace, kindness,*
    *and joy.*
*May I model living an expansive life,*
*by accepting all opportunities for cultivating growth,*
    *play,*
*and above all,*
*adventure.*

There is a word in the Akan language of Ghana, "sankofa," that encourages us to retrieve things of value from our past to help make positive progress to our futures. This new spark statement serves as a sankofa reminder. It urges me to remember where I came from, as I create and curate my future. It's a statement of not only what I believe but what I want to become.

*The first half of life is biography; the second half is autobiography.*

I thought of what I'd achieved in my past—education, career, parenting—and realized that while raising my daughter was one of the most challenging and rewarding things I'd done, it also necessarily meant that I'd suppressed some of my own curiosity and adventurous spirit. We parents often invest less time in our own pursuits in deference to raising our children.

It was time to reignite that inquisitiveness—not only because I owed it to myself, but because I owed it to Alex. It was time to model the experimentation and exploration that I hoped she would embrace as she began creating her own adult life. I hoped she would couple common sense and grounded confidence in what she had already accomplished with dreaming about an expansive future. If I wanted her to find courage to try everything that challenges her and grow in all ways that interest her, I needed to model that for her.

It was time to write my autobiography.

It was time to play.

# NINE

# Power Play

*What the hell am I doing here?*

It was 1998, and I was sitting on the edge of a sketchy boat, looking out at the watery expanse of the Sea of Cortez. My scuba tank was heavy on my back, and my fins felt tight around my ankles. Wild-eyed, I glanced over at my friend Donna.

This was all her fault. Three months earlier, she had convinced me to join her in a scuba-diving certification class. I didn't really have any excuse to turn her down. I'm from the Caribbean, for heaven's sake, home to some of the best diving in the world. It seemed ridiculous *not* to take the opportunity to get certified.

Many folks who refuse to attempt scuba diving cite the usual reasons: Surprise shark attacks. Rogue currents. The ever-present possibility of drowning. I will admit that these were all nagging fears when I signed up. In the very first class, I quickly learned that those nightmares were the least of my concerns. Decompression sickness, also known as "the bends," was a far more real and present danger: caused by returning to the surface too quickly, it can lead to painful injury or even death. With increasing horror, I paid close attention in every class, double- and triple-checking that I fully internalized every safety procedure and process. Even though I never grew comfortable breathing underwater, by some miraculous stroke of providence, I managed to pass my final open-water exams and earned my dive card. So to celebrate completing the class, Donna, who was the travel coordinator at the company where I worked, booked us a quick weekend dive trip a short flight away from Houston: Los Cabos.

Which is how I found myself sitting on the side of a rickety boat being pitched by rough waves under a blazing Mexican sun.

"It'll be fine," Donna whispered to me, just as the divemaster called out to our group.

"Let's go! In the water! Remember, stay with your dive buddy, and keep an eye on me." One by one, the four other divers on the boat entered the water.

Donna lowered her mask. "Come on," she said, before putting her regulator in her mouth and following suit.

I put on my mask and adjusted my buoyancy compensator. Placing my right hand on my mask and regulator, and my left hand on my weight belt, I scooted my butt back on the boat's edge. I looked over my shoulder to make sure that the other divers had swum out of the way.

*Here goes*, I thought, and rolled backward into the water.

The water was clear and chilly. I could see the group nearby, already descending into the deep blue. The divemaster had his eyes on me.

*Are you okay?* he signed.

*I'm okay.* I returned the sign and began deflating my buoyancy vest.

As I slowly sank, I felt a sharp twinge in my right ear. Descending into the ocean can cause the pressure in your ears to increase, leading to pain or discomfort similar to what you might feel when a plane takes off or lands. I put a shot of air in my vest and ascended about a foot. The stinging subsided.

*Are you okay?* The divemaster signed again.

I pointed to my ear and waggled my flattened palm side to side, using conventional diver sign language. By now, everyone had sunk to the ocean floor, about thirty feet below me. I could still see them pretty clearly, and I knew if they waited for me to join them, they'd be burning through the precious air in their tanks. *Let's just go,* I motioned to the divemaster. *I can follow along while I try to descend.*

*Okay,* he motioned, and signaled to the group to follow him. Frustrated, I made my way behind the group, now about twenty feet higher than they were. Luckily, below the surface, the water was calm, but I noted that I was still breathing quickly.

*Relax,* I thought. *Slow your breath.* I reminded myself that as long as I could still see the group, I was fine. Every now and then the divemaster would look up at me, and sign. *Are you okay?*

*I'm okay,* I'd respond, slowly, gingerly, attempting to descend a little deeper. I remained calm, and as I mindfully took slow, deep breaths, I began to enjoy myself a little. I marveled at the deep blue color of the water around me, the bubbles slowly rising from my dive companions below, and the cadence of my own breathing through my regulator. *Inhale . . . silence. Exhale . . . bubbles.* It was peaceful. It was meditative.

By this point, I was about twenty feet below the surface, and my companions were still just above the sea floor, now at about forty feet. Their pace had slowed, and a dark form appeared in the distance.

*What is that?* I wondered, squinting through my mask. The form grew bigger. My friends had stopped moving below me. *What is that? Oh, shit.*

The shape rushed toward me. My eyes grew huge, and I gasped.

Inches from my face, nose-to-dive-mask, was a big, beautiful sea lion.

I was frozen. The sea lion blinked at me. I'd stopped breathing, something you're never supposed to do during a dive. *Breathe*, I told myself, but I couldn't.

The sea lion shot away, and I exhaled, exhilarated. I looked down at the group, to see if they'd noticed, but they were busy having their own encounters with a raft of sea lions that had arrived. One of the animals snuck behind a diver unnoticed and nipped at his fins. When the diver started, the sea lion darted away, only to do it again when the diver turned his back. The divemaster was doing somersaults in the water, and another sea lion was mimicking him with her own tumbles. The remainder of our group watched, rapt, as the animals cavorted around them. Before long I realized that I had descended alongside my companions with no ear pain and no worries, delighting in these playful animals.

It felt as if time had stopped. All too soon, however, the divemaster interrupted our collective trance: it was time to surface. Dejected, we left the sea lions, slowly making our way back to where the boat was moored. We arrived topside (after a three-minute safety stop), and spat out our regulators, climbing aboard and excitedly talking over each other about what we had witnessed. I looked over at Donna, and she was grinning at me, her hair dripping, her eyes dancing.

The outboard engine of the unsteady boat revved, and we turned toward shore. During our remaining days in Mexico, there was a lightness and ease to each of our subsequent dives. Gone was any trepidation for the rest of our holiday. We never experienced the dance of the sea lions again, but the memory of their energy has remained with me ever since.

My friend Jeff Harry is a positive psychology consultant and leadership coach who has traveled around the world teaching individuals and organizations how to maximize their innovation and creativity. He has worked with huge corporations—think Microsoft, Google, Amazon, and Facebook—and has won awards as one of the top human resources influencers on the internet. His work has been featured in the *New York Times*, on CNN, and in the *San Francisco Chronicle*. And the coolest part is that Jeff has accomplished all of this through play.

"I define play as any joyful act where you forget about time, are fully present in the moment and let go of results," he explained to me. "And everyone's play looks different. Sometimes we get a myopic vision of what play is supposed to be. But play is whatever that thing is that puts you into flow—that thing that makes you come alive."

"I know that you teach a lot of companies how to incorporate play into their organizations, for the purpose of cultivating innovation and creativity," I said. "But why is it important to cultivate intentional play in our personal lives?"

"Well, often as adults, we live lives where we get hyper focused on results, and expectations are the thief of joy," he explained. "But when we play, our implicit mind—the part of our brain that learns unconsciously and causes us to behave in ways that we might not be aware of—shows up. It makes us highly creative. Instead of fixating on a result, we see all the opportunities for joy in front of us. We're open to all the possible adventures. Play gives us a shot of dopamine—that's why it feels so good—and maybe a little oxytocin, and serotonin, and some endorphins as well. You've probably felt this happen to you in the past, when you've traveled, and said things like, 'Yes, I'll hop on that moped! Yes, I'll go to that deserted island! Yes, I'll go to some random party to dance in the moonlight!' And then suddenly, you say to yourself, 'How did I get here?' You got there by playing and being open to saying yes."

When Jeff described how travel can inspire play, he didn't know about my sea lion story, but that experience instantly came to my mind. The sea lions were clearly playing with us, and we all—especially the dive master, with his somersaults in the water—were clearly playing back. But it never occurred to me to think of scuba diving as "play," especially since I was so anxious entering the water during that dive. Still, considering Jeff's definition, at a certain point I *did* lose track of time, and I certainly wondered how I managed to get myself in that situation. Could I have been truly *playing*?

If there is a bona fide expert of play, that person is Dr. Stuart Brown, a psychiatrist and founder of the National Institute for Play. He is also the author of the national bestseller *Play: How It Shapes the Brain, Opens the Imagination, and Invigorates the Soul*. In his book, Dr. Brown supports Jeff's assertion that everyone's play is different, further describing eight types of "play personalities." "As we grow older," he explains, "we start to have strong preferences for certain types of play over others." Dr. Brown discovered these play personalities in his research.

**Jokers** enjoy play that revolves around silliness, like telling jokes or even playing practical jokes.

For **Kinesthetes**, play involves movement. Kinesthetes include athletes, but also people who simply enjoy moving as part of dance, yoga, jump rope, swimming, walking, and so on.

**Explorers** prefer to play by seeking out new places, feelings, or learnings. They might play by traveling but also by enjoying new experiences or learning new subjects.

**Competitors** enjoy competitive play: games with specific rules, playing to win.

**Directors** enjoy planning and executing scenes and events. They're the party-givers, the friend-getaway organizers.

For **Collectors**, collecting objects or experiences are sources of play. These are the folks who, for example, collect classic cars. Or my friend Susan, who is passionate about penguins: she and her husband have traveled across the globe to visit all eighteen species of penguin in their natural habitats. (Who knew there were eighteen species of penguin?)

**Artist/Creators** play by making things: painting, print-making, pottery, furniture-making, knitting, sewing, taking things apart and putting them back together. They play using their hands to create.

And finally, **Storytellers** play not only by telling stories but also igniting their imaginations through reading books, watching movies, or even pretending and acting.

Identifying your play personality is helpful because intentional play is an integral part of living well. "Everyone notices when a friend's hair turns gray in their forties, and the wrinkles accumulate in the fifties, but the friend usually has the same personality and is just as sharp as ever mentally," writes Dr. Brown. "But I've noticed that the brain really begins to change in the sixties and seventies, and some people start to lose the intellectual sharpness they had before. The people who stay sharp and interesting are the ones who continue to play."

I'd never considered play as an integral part of self-care as we age, but it makes sense. After reading

Dr. Brown's words, I tried to identify which of the play personalities he described resonated with me. My Hula-Hooping and jump-roping habits invoke my inner kinesthete, and given that I'm a writer, it's no surprise that storytelling is a source of enjoyment for me. But I suspect my most dominant play personality is that of the explorer. Becoming a certified diver, venturing out in a precarious boat in a foreign land, even meeting and making new friends against the walls of the Palais des Papes in the south of France: those are the times that really made my heart sing.

My friend Steve Bennett—the travel guru of the "thirty minutes for me" philosophy in chapter 4—has a strong opinion about why that might be. "The thing about adventure travel," says Steve, "is that you learn so much about yourself, and how you relate to other people when you're in situations that are completely out of your comfort zone and maybe even a little bit dangerous. You learn to see things differently and relate to people differently. You surprise yourself."

Steve was a teenager when his mother passed away, and he said he sometimes thinks about all the things that he has gotten to do and see that she never had the chance to do and see. "We're not in control of when our time comes, so why waste any time worrying about it?" he asked. "Travel allows me to let go and allow amazing things to happen, and let my life play out in ways that surprise and excite me. I'm sure that I'll be doing some form of adventure and exploration, in one way or another, for the rest of my life."

As Steve describes, travel is one of the primary ways to scratch an exploration itch, but it's not the only way. Dr. Brown explains that exploration "can be emotional—searching for a new feeling or deepening of the familiar, through music, movement, or flirtation.

Or it can be mental: researching a new subject or discovering new experiences and points of view."

My friend Asha Dornfest, a writer, has a similar thirst for exploration. She often hits the road for solo trips up and down the western coast of America. But when the last of her kids left home for college, she did something else unexpectedly adventurous: she went back to school. "I didn't go back to school with a plan of pursuing any degree," she explained, "and I chose undergraduate classes for the very practical reason that there's an inexpensive college ten minutes away from my house."

"So why *did* you go back?" I asked.

"Well, at that point we had been experiencing pandemic isolation for quite some time," she said. "I'm a person who really thrives in collective environments, and I wanted to be in a place with other people where we were all doing something together. I wanted a communal experience. Back when I was eighteen and first went to college, I was almost an English major, but I ended up being a sociology major. This time, I felt the pull to return to the realm of literature and art. I was wrestling with questions of meaning and purpose and realized humans have been asking questions about meaning and purpose for thousands of years. I could have read a bunch of spiritual texts I didn't particularly want to read, or I could go read all the great novels and books that tackled these questions. And since I learn best through conversation, it seemed obvious that I should go to school, where I could discuss these ideas with professors and fellow students."

"But you already have a college degree. Did you ever consider a graduate program?"

"But why would I do that, especially when I could very easily and cheaply take undergraduate courses? Graduate school is expensive! I would have had to apply, I would've had to take graduate admissions tests . . . that's a lot of work! And my goal wasn't to earn another degree, I just wanted to take a few courses. Besides, there was a part of me that remembered how amazing college campuses are, and taking a few classes was a simple way to experience that energy of a college campus again."

"Didn't it feel weird to likely be the oldest student in the class?"

"Well, honestly, I feel super comfortable around people that age, so I had no qualms about walking into a college classroom where everybody was twenty-two or maybe even nineteen. And there were a couple of other people my age, looking awkward. But I just walked in, sat down, and became a student! I just figured that I belonged there, because I *like* people who are younger than me and who were different from me. I felt like I could learn something from the conversation. I wanted to be a learner again."

After a semester's worth of classes, Asha reevaluated. Because of the pandemic, she had been apart from her mother and extended family for a while, and realized she wanted to spend the next few months with her far-flung family, now that they could gather again. But it was impossible to reconnect and attend class at the same time, so she didn't re-enroll for the next quarter. Nowadays, Asha writes a popular newsletter about being a parent to adults. "Did the experience of going back to school help shape any of the work you're doing now and what you're hoping to create going forward?" I asked her.

"Absolutely," she said. "Being back in college reinforced my belief in art as a tool and vehicle for social change. My classes—including one on rhetoric, which is the study of persuasive language—gave me a way to talk about social change. The professors used articles, treatises, books, and plays as case studies, and showed how their content had the power to shift thinking. I have an allergy to giving advice, but I'm a fine writer, I believe in storytelling, and I excel at creating community conversation. I'm committed to using these abilities to create a space for parents of adults. Taking those classes allowed me to feel more confident with those skills, and I was able to practice them within the context of the class, with classmates who were wildly different from me. The experience gave me new ways to interact with theoretical ideas and make them concrete. It reinvigorated my ability to focus, write on command, and cultivate skills in both listening and participating well. I use all these skills in the community I'm creating for parents of adults."

The idea that going back to school for a semester was enough to help bring clarity to the work Asha wanted to do in the future: well, I loved it. Clearly, continual learning works for her. I asked her if she could articulate why that is.

Asha thought for a moment. "It's an interesting paradox: there's a certain part of us that remains the same, a core part of us, and there's a part of us that changes based on the experiences that we have. As we change—and stay the same—the world continues to change as well. When we pursue learning, we're offering ourselves to the world as it is and as we are. I believe there's this endless energy in the world that is available for us to tap into at any point, and in so many ways. When we plug ourselves into that—whether it's by having a new experience, or slightly expanding what we thought we were capable of doing, or meeting a new friend, or creating a new relationship—it reminds us of what we're still capable of, and it brings energy to everything else."

"And it's not just about going to college," she clarified. "Meeting new people, whether it's through taking a class or any other new experience, makes your life richer. The energy that comes from continuing to learn or experiencing new things lights up every corner of your life. It makes things possible that you didn't think were possible before. I had to try different things so I could figure out what resonates with me now. Some of it was stuff that had resonated with me in the past, but some of it took me completely by surprise. These are the experiences that keep me living and growing."

Laura Mayes, the friend who commented about my pilot light at the beginning of this book, has a similar outlook on being a continual learner. Laura's varied career has spanned from being a high school English teacher to a public relations executive to an Emmy-award-winning writer to the creator of a huge annual social media conference to the director of two of the most popular podcasts in the world. Now Laura has embarked on possibly the most unexpected project of all: producing a musical.

"It appears that you are not a person who is afraid to try new things," I said.

"I am not," she grinned. "Not at all. My filter for deciding to do something is: 'Is it fun or is it not fun?'"

"Is that true?"

"Pretty much—or at least 'is it interesting?' I mean, if it's not interesting, it's not going to be fun, and if it's not fun, it's not going to be interesting. So those two things are kind of connected for me."

While I loved how this sounded, I had to admit: this sort of filter also seemed a bit risky. I can think of a lot of interesting, fun things to do that would end up bankrupting me. "Haven't you ever needed to do something for reasons more practical than 'it's fun'?" I asked.

"Oh, I make practical decisions, just not at the expense of them being fun or interesting," Laura answered. "In hindsight, I see this outlook was modeled by my parents: They each had varied careers, without a particular path. They did what was interesting to them, and if it stopped being interesting, they switched. I saw them find something they liked and do it, and I also saw them find things they didn't like to do and get out of it."

Laura told me that when she was a teenager and adults asked her what she wanted to do when she grew up, her mother would interrupt, saying, "Why are you asking her that? I don't even know what I want to do when *I* grow up!" Her parents didn't pressure her to accomplish any particular thing by any particular age. "The rule in our house was work hard, contribute, and don't whine—nothing more. There was never any pressure about succeeding in any particular way. Because of this, I've always been curious and a hard worker, but I never felt any stress about failing, because even if I failed at something, at least I tried."

"This makes sense," I said. "But seriously, you've done some *wildly* different things. Do they have *anything* in common, or am I missing something?"

"Well, story has always been important to me," she said. "I think the throughline of my work is that everything I do is about telling or amplifying untold stories, creating connections, and putting as much love and creativity into the world as I can. Working for the PR company, I amplified stories. As the founder of a social media conference that began specifically when women began taking up blogging as a medium of self-expression, I amplified stories. As a director of two podcasts, I shared stories. And now as a producer of a musical based on the life of a real person, I'm amplifying his story. It's why, I think, I'm not afraid to fail, because even if I fail, the world will be better because we *tried*. In just the attempt, even if I fail, someone will have heard or experienced or connected with the story."

"It still seems really brave to try," I insisted. "How do you know that you're going to be able to handle these projects?"

"First of all, for most of these projects, I'm doing them with someone else. I'm rarely going it alone. Second, I'm a hard worker, and I am confident that I will always carry my own weight. And finally, I get creative juice from learning. When I tackle something new—like the podcasts, for example, or the musical—I go in *deep*. I didn't know anything about podcast production before I started, so I read every book I could about the subject, and I now have a full library on how to create a podcast. When a friend, who has strong relationships in the world of entertainment, told me a story one evening, I immediately said, 'That's a musical! You should make that musical.' And she said, 'Let's do it together.' It sounded interesting and fun, so now I have so many books on musicals, I could earn a master's degree in Broadway shows. I deeply believe you can do anything with a good library card," she finished with a grin.

I agreed, but I probed further. "Do you ever have any self-doubt about getting too old to try new things?"

"No." She made a face before laughing out loud. "*No*. If anything, the possibility of failure has become even *more* inconsequential. I figure that as we get older, we take all the lessons of the past forward with us. All our past experiences equip us for all our future adventures.

Besides, ten years ago, if you were to ask me if I would ever produce a podcast, I would've responded, 'What's a podcast?' The world changes so fast that new adventures open up to us every day that we could have never imagined would exist. So I'm just going to keep pushing things through this brain of mine as long as I can. The right path will always find me if I'm open to it. And I can't wait to see what else the world puts in front of me."

Laura's joy-filled curiosity is a way of life for her. But the cultivation of a play practice can also be instrumental in helping us during major life transitions. Writer Michelle Fishburne's life is proof of this. Her story involves a Target parking lot, an unlikely mode of travel, and a speech about a chicken suit.

In 2020, Michelle Fishburne was facing a doozy of a transition. At the beginning of the year, she suddenly lost some of her hearing and most of her balance. By spring, she was laid off from her beloved public relations job working for an organization she deeply believed in when the COVID pandemic had rendered her position obsolete. Come June, her youngest had graduated from high school, making her officially an "empty-nester." At the end of July, she still had not secured employment, despite heroic efforts. To make matters worse, the lease on her house was ending. With no job, nowhere to live, and life looking a bit hopeless, she decided to do the only reasonable thing she could.

She played.

"I was sitting in the parking lot of a Target, trying to make a very basic decision," Michelle shared with me. "I needed to figure out where to tell the movers to move all my belongings. I didn't want to rent a place, because I had no idea where I was going to live. I had been applying for jobs all over the country and hadn't received a bite yet. I had been applying for months, for jobs that were going again and again to people who were younger than me. I applied for jobs that were way below my pay level. I was offering to *volunteer* for organizations, and still not getting any gigs. I was desperate."

But then, Michelle told me, she remembered something that a yoga teacher had once said to her: *Whenever there is scarcity, there is also abundance.* "So I tried to focus on what I *did* have," she said. "And the first thing that came to mind was my RV."

Michelle comes from a long line of caravanning folk. During the Great Depression in the 1930s, when Michelle's maternal grandfather lost his job, he moved his family into a travel trailer. "I have an article that was written about them at the time, and in the accompanying photograph, my grandparents are all dressed up and they're making tea in their trailer," she said, grinning. "They talk about how eventually they hoped to have a house again, but for the time being, they were enjoying this unexpected way of life."

Then, many decades later, when Michelle's parents retired from their jobs, *they* moved into a motor home, and for seven years they traveled around the country as professional photographers. In 2006, Michelle bought her own motor home, and she and her kids joined her parents on the road. During that time, she homeschooled her children.

So sitting there in that Target parking lot, trying to figure out where to have the movers take her belongings, Michelle said she realized she already had deep confidence in her ability to make her way through the world with her motor home. "And obviously, it was a cheap way to live while I didn't have a job," she said.

"So, you decided to travel," I said.

"Yes, but there was more," she told me. "I knew that I had the motor home, but I also knew that even though I could go to somewhere beautiful, like the beach, it would just make me sad because my kids weren't with me to enjoy it. But then I thought, 'Wait a minute. I could put together a project that has some visibility, and it could serve as proof-of-concept of what I'm capable of, my ability to create something out of nothing.' It could help me gain employment. I'm really curious about the world and people, and my parents had taught me photography during my time with them. As a public relations executive, I knew how to write, I understood media, and I knew how to get press. So I decided to do a project interviewing and photographing people, and I called it 'Americans of the Pandemic.' I knew that my own experience of loss during 2020 would help me better understand the loss others had to be feeling because of the pandemic. And so I set off."

Michelle's project was a huge success. It was covered by national and international media, and it landed her a book deal—and eventually, a job.

"This was so smart of you," I said. "How the hell did the idea occur to you?"

"It's a lesson I actually learned when I was in high school," she said, grinning. "I was at a speech team competition, and part of the tournament required extemporaneous speaking. We had to draw pieces of paper out of a hat, and whatever random phrase was on the paper was the topic we had to speak about. When I drew my slip of paper out of the hat, all it said was, 'How do I get out of this chicken suit?'"

I laughed.

"In the moment, I decided to use the sentence as a metaphor for how to get out of a tough situation. Years later, while I was on the road for what became my book, *Who We Are Now: What Americans Lost and Found during the COVID-19 Pandemic*, I remembered that tournament topic. And I realized that I had, indeed, gotten out of the chicken suit! It just took reminding myself where my abundance was in the middle of scarcity, and where I found my joy. By tapping into those things, I was able to access an expanded view of all the opportunities that lay ahead. That's not to say that once I set out on my trip, I was confident it was going to all work out; I wasn't. But I do believe that the antidote to fear is action. And day by day, mile by mile, the fear began to subside."

Michelle is an explorer but also a collector, amassing tales of resilience around America as part of her play. And while I've no intention of RV-ing anytime soon, her lessons for how to tap into a play mindset during times of transition are really powerful. Remember abundance. Remember that action is an antidote to fear. Remember what you are capable of. These seemed like mantras to remember as I entered this new phase of life.

A few weeks after we'd dropped our daughter at university, the oppressive Texas summer heat finally broke. Marcus and I were establishing a new, child-free routine, but I realized that our twentieth wedding anniversary had come and gone. It had passed while we were in Chicago, eclipsed by all the excitement of moving Alex to her new home. Having been fully enchanted by the tiny cabin where I'd stayed a few months earlier on my mini-sabbatical, I knew that taking my camping-loving husband Marcus back for a visit might be the perfect way to celebrate. So on a whim, we packed up our dog and a few bags and headed north to the cabins for a short stay.

Our car pulled up to our home for the next two nights. The burn ban that was in place when I'd come earlier in the summer had been lifted, and after we unpacked the car, Marcus stared a campfire to cook our dinner. We sat watching the flames, drinking wine and chatting. Marcus could not stop casting amused glances my way. Unlike me, he thrives in the outdoors. He grew up on the Cornish coast of rural southwest England, in a family who camped often. A kinesthete by nature, Marcus loves play that involves terrifying feats on mountain bikes and surfboards. One of his favorite vacations as a single person was a trailbike tour through Morocco, where he slumbered under the stars in a sleeping bag that had to be shaken upon waking, lest a snake or spider had cozied up to him during the night.

My idea of hell, in other words. So the fact that we were sitting outside, cooking our food over a campfire, tickled him to no end.

The sun began setting. "I wonder what Alex is doing," he said, his eyes never leaving the campfire. Marcus and Alexis have a close relationship, and I knew he was missing his shopping buddy.

"Living her best life, I imagine," I said. Her social media feeds had been full of images of her Chicago dorm room being Ground Zero for hangouts, animated evidence of her and her new friends exploring the city, and general glimpses of joyful college life.

"It's weird, isn't it?" I said to Marcus, suddenly missing Alex myself. "Just the two of us again. We haven't had that for eighteen-and-a-half years."

"No, we haven't," he smiled.

"Doesn't this worry you?" Of the two of us, I am, hands-down, the champion worrier, while Marcus is unflappable. "We have less than two years' experience in life just being about the two of us. Also, that was *twenty years ago*. There's no way that we're the same people we were back then. What if we don't work without a kid to raise?"

He narrowed his eyes. "What the hell is wrong with you?" he asked. "We're going to work. We *work*. Why wouldn't we work?"

I ignored him. "I know what we need," I said. "We need a *project*. Raising a child was a big-ass project. We need another project."

He stared at me for a moment. And then he returned his attention to the campfire. "You know what I'd love to do?" he said quietly. "I'd like to learn to sail."

"Really?!" At first, I was surprised. But then I remembered: Marcus's first job after high school was working as a cook on a live-aboard dive boat in England. The way he tells it, when he first got the gig at age eighteen, he would spend long days being seasick while the crew and their customers went diving in the frigid waters off Cornwall. When they returned to the boat, Marcus would cook their dinner. He has always looked back at that time living on the boat with great fondness, despite the fact that he earned only £125 per week for nine months. ("About £1 an hour," he says with a grin.) While he might have been criminally underpaid, he remains a stellar cook and I am the grateful beneficiary of his culinary skills most nights of the week.

"Huh. Sailing," I murmured. As different as Marcus and I are, the one thing that we have in common is that we both grew up in small communities near the ocean (even though they were 4,200 miles apart). We share a deep love of the sea, and the more I thought about it, the more appealing the idea of learning how to sail became. Reeling in sails and tacking into the wind would be attractive to my kinesthete husband; sailing to new destinations would certainly make my inner explorer come alive.

"Then we should sail," I said. "We should look into lessons. That could actually be really fun."

I remembered what my friend Jeff told me one time when I asked him why we should all play as we get older. He was surprised that I would even ask. "Karen, that's like asking me why we should love as we get older, or eat as we get older, or even pursue what brings us joy as we get older. We should play because those fun, joy, play moments that result are what makes life worth living. Why shouldn't we be focused on creating as many of those moments as we can?"

He leaned forward to emphasize his next point. "Here's the secret to living a long life," he said. "Give yourself permission to play every day. Not only will you increase your chances of living a long life; you'll likely experience a more fulfilling, fun-filled, fantastical ride of a life, one that you'll appreciate so much more."

I thought of Jeff's words while I stoked the campfire. Marcus reclined in the Adirondack chair next to mine. Together, we sat silently, dreaming of sailing sunlit seas and watching sparks from the flames soar into the Texas sky.

# Epilogue: Kaleidoscope

A funny thing happens when you write a book about joyful aging.

You go into it assuming it will be a relatively easy book to write. "Don't worry about aging!" you'll quip. "It's no big deal! I promise!" You'll share stories from various experts and friends, counting on their words to illuminate the fact that aging is simply the evolution of who we *are* into who we're going to *become*. Easy-peasy.

But then you learn how naive you are.

You learn about the anti-aging forces trying to capitalize on our discomfort with getting older (to the tune of *trillions* of dollars, remember). You learn about internalized ageism, and all the ways that societal links between youth and happiness have gotten into your head. You learn about the effort required to be content with becoming who you want to become. You learn that aging isn't for the faint of heart, nor is it "easy-peasy."

But then again, evolution rarely is.

I mentioned at the beginning of this book that I've always been pretty optimistic about getting older. Now that I've written this book, I find I'm even *more* so. I still maintain that what's wonderful about aging eclipses what is challenging about it. I'm more convinced than ever that we each have the power to create and curate our own futures. And I still believe that despite the trials that aging may bring, gifts will arise as well. With some effort and intention, joy can be the inevitable by-product of getting older.

Maryjane Fahey has collected impressive evidence of this. Maryjane is an author and creative director and the powerhouse behind GloriousBroads.com, a site of images and stories that take on patriarchy, ageism, and racism while celebrating and elevating "broads of all bodies."

"I started the site, featuring these glorious broads, because I was attracted to the 'unconventionalism' that they held in their hearts," Maryjane told me. "They've aged imaginatively. These are women who are making their own rules. I'm very attracted to their radicalness, the way they aren't bound by some sort of timeline that society puts on them."

"I love this, and I've so enjoyed following the women you feature on the site," I said to her. "But how do you think they cultivate that radicalness? What's their secret?"

"Well, there's also a joy that comes with aging," she answered. "Not every part of aging, of course—but the joy's there. I think their radicalness comes from tapping into that joy. Doing so takes a commitment to yourself—health, breath, spirit, everything—and requires constant self-love. But if you make that commitment to yourself, well, aging can be a joyous trip."

Defy society's expectations of aging. Be imaginative. Define what it means to get older by prioritizing joy. Commit to constant self-love: I think Maryjane is onto something, evidenced in my own experience as I wrote this book. By applying the wisdom of the folks who I interviewed, I've gotten an up-close-and-personal glimpse of what this radicalness—this *rebellion*—can look like. I got curious about my health, working with an equally curious doctor and digging deep into my own numbers, taking control of how my body feels. I curated and created how I want to appear in the world, free from societal expectations or so-called beauty "ideals." I've clarified my mission and purpose, and reclaimed play and adventure. I move and I rest. In short, over the months of writing this book, I've cultivated practices of self-care.

Through all of this, I'm reminded of a critical discovery, one that I made when I glanced at myself in that bathroom mirror four years earlier: it can be very easy to conflate "old" and "stressed." Before that revelation, I had prioritized life's challenges over self-care and self-compassion—a rookie mistake. The purpose of self-care isn't solely for recovery. In fact, I would argue that it's the other way around: it's through nurturing our whole selves that we gather the energy to meet life head-on. And when we fail to do it . . . well, the stress shows on our bodies. So when I saw my reflection, my knee-jerk reaction was that the stress I was seeing was due to my age, a clear indication that in my mind "old" meant "tired" or "run down." It was a flash of internalized ageism.

Because let's face it: no cream, serum, pill, food, or juice can reverse aging. Obviously. And the truth is that as I write these words four years later, I *do* look older, if my salt-and-pepper hair has anything to say about it. But because of this consistent practice of self-care and self-compassion over the past year, there's another difference in the way I look compared to the photo of my reflection I took four years ago. My eyes are brighter, I'm more energetic, and according to friends and family and even my doctor, there's a discernable *glow*.

And by the way, it's not an accident that these words—"glow," "bright," even "pilot light"—keep reappearing as metaphors. I believe there's a reason we use light words and phrases—such as "a brilliant smile" or "a sparkling personality" or "a radiant soul"—to describe people to whom we're drawn. We are referring to the light, the spirit, that animates each of us. Why wouldn't we want this light to be as bright as possible? Personally, I'm far more interested in being radiant than young. Radiant, after all, is timeless.

But what about when things go wrong? At the beginning of this book, I mentioned that I wouldn't be talking about some of the challenges that come with aging—there are enough books focused on those. Still, *not* discussing them doesn't change the fact that challenges may indeed arise. What then?

I'm reminded of a conversation a friend once shared with me. She had just endured a really difficult breakup, and she was spiraling into despair. "What if I never find love again?" she wailed to her therapist. Her therapist, a calm, no-nonsense woman, simply smiled at her and said, "You have evidence to suggest otherwise." I've kept this story close any time I'm facing a challenge and start to panic that I won't be able to handle it, and I shared it in *The Lightmaker's Manifesto*. It's such a powerful sentence that it deserves a spot in every book I ever write: *I have evidence to suggest otherwise.*

I suspect as we all think back on our lives, we can find evidence in our pasts of having weathered very difficult challenges, and we came out of those situations, if not unscathed, at least alive. In fact, in some cases, those challenges might have even made us stronger. While loss or difficulty or grief is never any fun, on the other side we have usually learned something about ourselves or how to handle crises: lessons that we can take with us for the next time we have to face a seemingly insurmountable obstacle. So when challenges arise (and they invariably do, no matter what your age), take a deep breath and remind yourself that you've faced difficult things before in ways that you can be proud of; therefore, you have evidence that you can do so again. *You can do this.*

Also remember, of course, that curiosity is key to light-filled aging. Curiosity will not only lead you to what it truly takes to nurture your body and your mind; it will also open portals to understanding your gifts, your skills, and even illuminate the values that are core to who you are and who you are to become. Curiosity can reveal exhilarating ways in which you can actualize your purpose. Curiosity is the basis of experimentation and adventure. Not to put too fine a point on it, but you will likely find that being curious—about yourself and the world around you—is a source of your joy.

And now, the final truth about joyful aging: it is never too late to act. Daniel Pink, author of the *New York Times* bestseller *The Power of Regret*, shares that as people get older, they tend to more deeply regret inaction (the things they never did) than action (the things they did). In fact, his data indicated that by age fifty, people expressed inaction regrets twice as often as action regrets, and that age was by far the strongest predictor of regrets of inaction. So when your curiosity leads you to something intriguing—whether it's writing that thank-you note, or going back to school, or starting a new hobby or business—never be afraid to take the tiniest step toward making it happen. And then another, and then another. See where your curiosity leads—even if it takes you to huge, mondo-beyondo, bigger-than-you-ever-thought-imaginable dreams. *Just keep going.*

Michelle Fishburne, my caravanning friend, said it best. When I asked her what she hoped for her future, she said, "I don't know. I like to think of my life as a kaleidoscope. You know, that kid's toy that has all of those colored pieces inside, and each time you turn it a fraction, the pieces fall into a different pattern, and you have a whole new, beautiful image? I think one of the things that's so wonderful is that we have the constant opportunity to slightly adjust our kaleidoscope view and discover so many new, different versions of ourselves."

I love the idea of a kaleidoscope as a symbol for the way we can approach how we age: with curiosity, a spirit of playfulness, and experimenting with slight adjustments, fully expecting a new revelation of a beautiful image. And so I share Michelle's hope for all of us: that as we age, in her words, we "turn our kaleidoscopes just a fraction, so that we tumble into the next beautiful iterations of ourselves."

Ultimately, no matter your age or stage in life, it all comes down to prioritizing the cultivation of deep, soulful, intimate joy, in the unique way that stirs your spirit. Ignore the ageist messages that dominate all forms of media. Stay curious and consistently focus on self-care, creating and curating your own future self. Because in a world that capitalizes on our despair and disillusionment about ourselves, joy is the ultimate act of resistance.

And remember: kaleidoscopes work best when we point them toward the light.

# The Radiant
# Rebellion Toolkit

As you read this book, you likely noticed that I turn to my notebook to work through questions that I want to wrestle with. Over the past few decades, I've found that my notebook is the best way to tap into the inner wisdom I've gained as I've made my way through life. I'm confident that you, too, have an inner wisdom that can help you turn the kaleidoscope to illuminate your own path to your emerging, continually evolving, radiant self.

To that end, the following pages include everything you need to create your own Radiant Rebellion. You'll find Articles of Engagement—guidelines for fighting ageist beliefs, against others and yourself—as well as journal prompts to work through in a notebook. Essentially, you'll be creating your own Radiant Rebellion Handbook. Here are some recommendations for how to get started.

1. You'll need a notebook: any notebook will do, but I'd recommend finding one that is big enough to write all your reflections in, but small enough that you can carry it with you (because you never know when brilliance might strike). Also, find a pen that feels good to write with. Again, this doesn't have to be expensive—a drugstore pen will work fine—but you'll want one that's a joy to use.

2. The Radiant Rebellion Articles of Engagement that follow are designed to be removed from this book and glued to the inside cover of your notebook. You don't have to do this, of course, but having it inside the cover may be a helpful reminder of the mindset you're hoping to cultivate as you create your handbook.

3. One of the first things that you'll be doing is creating a Radiant Rebellion mantra: a short phrase to keep in mind as you proceed through the prompts. Keep the first page of your notebook blank so that once you've come up with your mantra, you can write it on that front page, to set the tone for all your future writing.

4. When doing the prompts, simply write stream-of-consciousness. Don't worry about perfect grammar or spelling. Remember, no one needs to see your notebook but you, and the point is to get your thoughts on paper. This handbook is for you, by you.

5. Take your time going through the prompts. There's no need to do them all in one sitting, and you may find over time you want to return to some of the prompts to add more thoughts or amend what you've recorded. You may even want to do the prompts out of order: One day, you might be moved to work on your spark statement, the next on internalized ageism. Whatever works. Also, your notebook shouldn't be something precious. I often doodle in my notebook, hand-letter quotes that I find inspiring, even glue in articles from magazines that give me food for thought, and that I can journal about later. Make the notebook work for you.

That's it! Enjoy tending to your pilot light, and welcome to the Radiant Rebellion. Let's raise a little hell.

# Articles of Engagement

**We are the Radiant Rebellion.**

We believe in defining who we are, and who we are to be,
taking the lessons of our pasts as we create our futures.
We are the authors of our own biographies.

We trust growing older is more expansive than the world would
have us believe.
We commit to speaking of and to ourselves and others
with age-positive kindness and respect.

We believe in nourishing the health within us.
Joyful movement is our way.

We believe in proud self-expression, through our words, manner,
and attire,
creatively telling and illustrating our values and histories.

We believe in the power of connection and belonging, to ourselves and to others.
We commit to spiritual self-care, the practice of gratitude, and
the expression of heartfelt appreciation to those who touch our lives.

We believe in play. We strive to live big every day.
We are confident in our ability to handle future challenges,
because of our rich history of handling them in our past.
We approach life with a sense of adventure.

**And we believe in a kaleidoscopic, light-filled future
to come.**

---

# Guide for Creating
# a Radiant Rebellion
# Handbook

The following are the prompts for writing your own Radiant Rebellion Handbook. They are organized by chapter, under the headings **Ignite**, **Disrupt**, **Connect**, and **Envision**, mirroring the book, should you choose to refer to the text for inspiration. I would recommend starting each prompt on its own page. And don't forget to take your time: Allow yourself to mull over your answers. I wouldn't do more than one prompt in any twenty-four-hour period, minimum.

## PART I: IGNITE

### Chapter 1 Call for Revolution

1. **Ask yourself: What are some of the preconceived notions I have held about aging?** As you read the first chapter of this book, were there any facts or statistics that surprised you? How, if at all, have they changed the way you think about aging?

2. **Ask yourself: What role do I hope to play in the Radiant Rebellion?** In an ideal world, how would you represent the Rebellion? Would you change the way you

approach life? Would you model what it means to get older to younger folks? Would you engage in more formal forms of anti-ageism activism? Take some time to brainstorm how you would shift your own outlook to embrace the Radiant Rebellion philosophy.

## Chapter 2 Pilot Light

1. **Ask yourself: Who do I see myself being?** Imagine it's twelve months from today and you're looking at yourself in the mirror. Who is the person you hope is looking back? Write your answers as fully as possible, and in the present tense (such as: "I am strong and resilient and doing meaningful work"). As you write, consider the following:

   > how you talk to yourself
   > how you take care of your body and health
   > how you express yourself through your attire and hobbies
   > how you care for your spirit
   > how you embody your meaning and purpose
   > how you nurture your relationships
   > the adventures you hope to be having

2. **Write your Radiant Rebellion Mantra.** As you review everything you've written in response to the question above, what word or phrase comes to mind that describes the person in your future reflection? This is your Radiant Rebellion Mantra. You could think of this book's subtitle as a mantra: "Reclaim aging. Practice joy. Raise a little hell." Write your personal word or phrase in the front page of your manual, and refer to it as you continue working on the rest of the prompts in creating this handbook.

3. **Ask yourself three bonus questions.** Begin a practice of asking yourself the following three questions every day for twenty-one days:

How can I feel healthy today?
How can I feel connected today?
How can I feel purposeful today?

As you come up with the answers (in your notebook or otherwise), include them your to-do list for the day.

At the end of twenty-one days of focusing on the answers to these questions, do you notice any trends? Is there any one activity that makes you feel particularly healthy, connected, and/or purposeful? Make a note of your answers.

## PART II: DISRUPT

### Chapter 3 Age of Rebellion

1. **Ask yourself: What do I think it means to "be young"?** What traits of "being young" are attractive to you? Brainstorm all the traits you attribute to "being young." (Some common ones are: curious, playful, active, adaptable, fun-loving.) Once you've made your list, consider how you can infuse more of your life with these traits. Consider how any of these lend themselves to helping you answer your bonus question of the previous prompt: What can you do today that taps into these traits to help you feel healthy, connected, or purposeful?

2. **Ask yourself: What are the gifts that living to my current age has given me?** Consider education, experience, street smarts, worldview: anything you view as a gift. Make a list of those gifts.

3. **Ask yourself: How can I be kinder?** Now that you know that you've been immersed in cultural ageism since you were young, how do you vow to be kind to yourself when it comes to how you view your own aging? Examples might include describing yourself to younger people as "older" rather than "old"; double-checking to see if there's a causal relationship for aches or forgetfulness that aren't related to age; becoming more precise with your language (instead of "I don't feel old," replace the word *old* with the word you really mean: *tired, unsexy, bored*). Reflect on this commitment to kindness in your notebook.

## Chapter 4 Body Politics

1. **Ask yourself: How do I love to move?** What are the ways you've loved moving in the past? Think back to childhood, if necessary: Roller-skating? Hula-Hooping? Playing soccer? Jump-roping? What was it you loved about those activities? Are there any activities you'd love to begin doing again? How can you replicate the feeling you had doing those activities now? Brainstorm all the ways these activities were/are fun for you (consider things like cadence, the ability to be outside, and the ability to be on a team).

2. **Ask yourself: How can I take thirty minutes for myself?** As you consider the bonus question related to health from chapter 2, what is something you can do today to dedicate *thirty minutes* to your health? Choose movement, or meditation, or even a nap—whatever will help you feel healthier today. Try to devote these thirty minutes to yourself for the next twenty-one days.

3. **Ask yourself: How can I nourish the health already inside me?** Over the next twenty-one days, what food can you *add* to your diet to make you feel healthy? It might be more water, or more fruit or vegetables, or even a small

snack, especially if you're in the habit of skipping meals. Consider how your choices would change if you viewed food as nurturing the health you already have inside you.

## Chapter 5 Beauty Myth

1. **Ask yourself: How will people know I have entered the room?** Return to the words you wrote in the first prompt, about the person you imagine will be looking back at you in the mirror a year from now. What is that person wearing that tells you they embody who you imagined them to be? As you write your answer to this question, consider colors, fabrics, and accessories.

2. **Curate your wardrobe.** It's time to shop your closet. What items do you already own that reflect your answer to the question above? What items can you donate? Do you own any items that you've not worn much or at all that reflect the person you imagine yourself becoming? Are there new ways or combinations to wear items you already have?

3. **Experiment with expression.** Now that you've curated your closet, for the next twenty-one days, practice adding or wearing items of clothing and accessories that make you feel like the person you imagined. At the end of the day, note if the color, outfit, or accessory affected how you moved through your day.

## PART III: CONNECT

## Chapter 6 Soul Fire

1. **Ask yourself: Where am I aware of my place in the world?** When do you feel most connected to something bigger than yourself: The mountains? The forest? Near the ocean? Early morning? Sunset? Church or temple?

Write down how you feel when you're in these places. How can you make these places more present in your life?

2. **Begin a meditation practice.** In the mornings during the next twenty-one days, take ten minutes to meditate. Set the timer on your phone for ten minutes, and then sit somewhere that is quiet and comfortable. Close your eyes or soften your gaze. Slow your breath: inhale slowly, pause, exhale, pause, repeat. As thoughts enter your mind, simply notice them, and then return your attention to your breathing.

After ten minutes, grab your notebook and journal: How do you feel? What physical sensations did you notice? Where did your mind wander? Then set an intention for yourself for the day ahead.

## Chapter 7 Radiant Alliance

1. **Develop a cadence of appreciation.** For the next twenty-one days, before starting your day, send a thank-you email or text to someone, simply expressing a small appreciation. It could be to a coworker for an insight they shared during a meeting, or to your partner for listening to you as you shared your day, or to a friend for joining you for coffee.

2. **Create regular "playdates" with your close friends.** Think about those local friends who are your ride-or-dies—the ones you can count on. If possible, see if you can check in with each other on a regular basis. Some ideas from friends of mine:

> My friend Nilofer is a huge fan of the walk-and-talk. Not only does she meet local friend to catch up as she walks; sometimes she calls me (I live thousands of miles away), and we both walk trails near our homes while we catch up.

My friend Jeff meets one of his friends periodical-
ly to connect over egg rolls. They are on the quest
for the best egg rolls in town, and they meet at a
different place every time to compare. The point,
of course, is for them to stay connected, but that
they have yummy egg rolls every time they meet
makes their time together that much more delicious.

3. **Launch a full Thank-You Project.** Consider writing
letters of gratitude to those who have helped, shaped, or
influenced you over the years. You can read more about
how my friend Nancy Davis Kho managed her project in chapter 7 for inspiration or pick up her book *The
Thank-You Project* for a deep dive. The most important
thing to remember is that writing the letters is more for
you, the writer, than your recipients. But trust me: your
recipients will be delighted too!

## PART IV: ENVISION

### Chapter 8 Mission Possible

1. **Brainstorm.** For this prompt, you will end up writing a
spark statement: a statement that embodies how you want
to move through the world for the years ahead. (You can
also read more about spark statements in my earlier book,
*The Lightmaker's Manifesto.*) To help you brainstorm, here
are some questions to answer in your notebook.

   a. Looking at your past, what were some of the biggest challenges you've faced? What did those challenges teach you? What are you most proud of
   having accomplished?

b.   What are you really good at? What are the things that you love to do so much that you would do them even if you never got paid to do them? What do people often thank you for?

c.   What issues are important to you now? What causes incite the most passion in you?

d.   If you could wave a magic wand, what is your vision for what you hope the world could be? Consider how this reflects on the issues that you're passionate about.

e.   What do you see as your mission? How could you advance the world in the direction of your vision? How can you use the things that you're really good at in service of that vision?

2.   **Write your Spark Statement.** Using your answers to the questions above, begin by writing sentences that encapsulate how you'll make your vision a reality, using the lessons of your past and the talents and gifts that you have. Your spark statement doesn't have to be long: aim for five sentences, but more or fewer is fine. It should capture who you are and who you aim to be. (And I'd love to hear what you come up with! Check out my website at karenwalrond.com and find the link entitled "spark statements." You can submit your spark statement and read what others have shared!)

## Chapter 9 Power Play

1.   **Ask yourself: How can I infuse more play into my life?** Think about the activities that you used to love doing when you were a kid. Can you do them now? Is there a hobby that you used to have that you'd love to take up again?

2. **Dust off dreams.** Think back over the years. What dreams have you shelved in the past? Make a list. Then consider what one small step you could take toward making them reality (such as education you might need, certifications you might earn). What would that one step be?

3. **Think mondo-beyondo dreams.** What big, audacious dreams would you like to try? Think of things that you might have never considered doing in the past that sound appealing now. How could you make them happen?

# Acknowledgments

I began writing this book because I was thinking about what it means to get older, but as I mentioned in the epilogue, I had no idea what I was getting into. Thank goodness I was surrounded by incredibly generous people whose support, encouragement, and wisdom were limitless. They made the writing process, while challenging, a true joy. These wonderful souls include:

The wise folks who took so much time out of their lives to meet with me, sometimes repeatedly, and endured my endless questions with such patience: Reeta Achari, Ashton Applewhite, Steve Bennett, Brené Brown, Tarana Burke, Ansley Collins Browns, Nancy Davis Kho, Asha Dornfest, Maryjane Fahey, Michelle Fishburne, Mike Gebremedhin, Jeff Harry, Katie Horwitch, Mira Jacob, Giyen Kim, Linda Lorelle, Laura Mayes, Brad Montague, Attillah Springer, Stasia Stavasuk, Tuhina Verma Rasche, Kermitt Walrond, and Karen Williams. *Thank you all.* Trust that even if your words don't appear in this book, the wisdom that you shared so freely was instrumental to the evolution of its final form.

Alice Bradley, my friend and book coach extraordinaire who kept poking and prodding at early drafts of this book and challenged me to go deep with my personal stories: even though getting vulnerable was really uncomfortable, you were always right. Valerie Weaver-Zercher, your superpower of being unfailingly kind while pulling no punches is awe-inspiring, as is your brainstorming tenacity. I'm so grateful to have such a wonderful editing partner in this book.

Pamela Blosch and Donna Abbott: Thank you for pushing me out of my comfort zone those many years ago. Because of you, I learned lessons of connection and play that will stay with me for the rest of my life.

Jessica Ashley, Amy Branger, Asha Dornfest, Justine Fanarof, A'Driane Nieves, Christine Koh, Mark Savage: thank you for your friendship, for recommending amazing people to speak with and sending related resource articles to read, and for generally being my cheering section.

To my parents, Kermitt and Yvette Walrond: thank you for modeling and embodying the spirit of the Radiant Rebellion. I took copious notes. To my sister, Natalie Walrond: thanks for always being in my cheering section.

And to my Marcus, whose quiet, steadfast support is an unwavering and constant source of love, and my Alexis, who makes me laugh and laugh and laugh: I love you endlessly.

# Notes

## Chapter 1

4 ". . . to ward off the sight." Nora Ephron, *I Feel Bad About My Neck* (New York: Alfred A. Knopf, 2006), 6.

5 ". . . despite any physical ailments." Michael L. Thomas et al., "Paradoxical Trend for Improvement in Mental Health with Aging: A Community-Based Study of 1,546 Adults Aged 21–100 Years," *The Journal of Clinical Psychiatry* 77, no. 8 (2016): e1019–25. https://doi.org/10.4088/JCP.16m10671.

5 ". . . decade after decade." Fran Lowry, "Aging Is Associated with Better Mental Health," Medscape, August 25, 2016, https://tinyurl.com/yz3vfd7p.

5 "America is clearly aging." "2020 Profile of Older Americans—Administration for Community Living," US Department of Health and Human Services, 3, accessed January 19, 2023, https://tinyurl.com/2p46bcx2.

5 ". . . numbers are going *down*." "2020 Profile of Older Americans—Administration for Community Living."

5 ". . . options for wellness." "Dramatic Shift to Wellness Signals New Era for Senior Living Communities, Survey Finds," International Council on Active Aging, January 2019, https://tinyurl.com/4ky9hxh8.

6 ". . . particularly women, are improving." Paola Scommegna, "An Improved State of Aging in America," Population Reference Bureau, 2020, accessed January 19, 2023, https://tinyurl.com/32ahxr56.

6 ". . . in the same period." Emily Stewart, "How the Anti-Aging Industry Turns You into a Customer for Life," Vox, July 28, 2022, https://tinyurl.com/34pmfjam.

7 ". . . at around age *twenty-five*." Stewart, "How the Anti-Aging Industry Turns You into a Customer for Life."

7 "... use anti-wrinkle products." "Young Americans Are Already Worried About Looking Old," DigitalHubUSA, September 6, 2021, https://tinyurl.com/bdfrwdsh.

7 "... syringe or surgery." Stewart, "How the Anti-Aging Industry Turns You into a Customer for Life."

7 "... largely without regulation." Becca Levy, *Breaking the Age Code: How Your Beliefs About Aging Determine How Long & Well You Live* (New York: William Morrow, 2022), 36.

8 "... negative age beliefs." Levy, *Breaking the Age Code*, 93.

8 "... oneself based on age." "Kicking off a Global Conversation About Ageism: Launch of the First UN Global Report on Ageism," World Health Organization, March 18, 2021, https://tinyurl.com/u7c2kh5v.

9 "... 'insidious scourge on society.' " "Ageism Is a Global Challenge: UN," World Health Organization, March 18, 2021, https://tinyurl.com/39zp2b2u.

9 "... on the basis of age." Alana Officer and Vânia de la Fuente-Núñez, "A Global Campaign to Combat Ageism," *Bulletin of the World Health Organization* 96, no. 4 ,(2018): 295–96, http://dx.doi.org/10.2471/BLT.17.202424.

9 "... deep-rooted human rights violation." "World Losing Billions Annually to Age-Based Prejudice and Discrimination," United Nations Department of Economic & Social Affairs, 2021, https://tinyurl.com/ys6e2yzc.

9 "... movement and combat ageism." "World Losing Billions Annually to Age-Based Prejudice and Discrimination."

12 "... in which it can enrich us." Ashton Applewhite, *This Chair Rocks: A Manifesto Against Ageism* (New York: Celadon Books, 2019), 60.

## Chapter 2

22 "... in the form of older people." Laura Davidow Hirshbein, "Popular Views of Old Age in America, 1900–1950," *Journal of the American Geriatrics Society* 49, no. 11 (2001): 1555–60, https://doi.org/10.1177/1357034X08093571.

23 "... the abilities of children." Hirshbein, "Popular Views of Old Age in America, 1900–1950."

25 "... person who *is* this." James Clear, *Atomic Habits: An Easy & Proven Way to Build Good Habits & Break Bad Ones* (New York: Avery, 2019), 30.

## Chapter 3

33 ". . . so I am old, no question." Penelope Lively, *Dancing Fish and Ammonites: A Memoir* (New York: Viking Adult, 2014), 9.

33 ". . . just you wait." Lively, *Dancing Fish*, 150.

34 ". . . involve social and political upheaval." Applewhite, *This Chair Rocks*.

36 ". . . do better on memory tests, and live longer." Ashton Applewhite, "Let's End Ageism," TED Talk, 2017, https://tinyurl.com/2va7y7px.

36 ". . . half your life ahead of you." Jo Ann Jenkins, *Disrupt Aging: A Bold New Path to Living Your Best Life at Every Age* (New York: PublicAffairs, 2016), 13.

37 ". . . better for all our citizens." Jenkins, *Disrupt Aging*, 30.

38 ". . . perceptions about race and gender." Ashton, *This Chair Rocks*, 41.

41 ". . . forgetfulness, weakness and decline." Levy, *Breaking the Age Code*, 4.

42 ". . . impact the way we feel and act." Levy, 14.

43 ". . . even affecting our will to live." Becca R. Levy, "Eradication of Ageism Requires Addressing the Enemy Within," *The Gerontologist* 41, no. 5 (October 1, 2001): 578–79, https://doi.org/10.1093/geront/41.5.578.

43 ". . . with the most negative views." Levy, *Breaking the Age Code,* 93.

44 ". . . resources she shares on her website." Ashton Applewhite, This Chair Rocks (website), https://thischairrocks.com/.

45 ". . . their vitality, their curiosity, their potential." Levy, *Breaking the Age Code*, 188.

## Chapter 4

47 ". . . as I waited for Anna," Not her real name.

49 " 'Yes,' he says confidently. 'It is.' " Apocalypse Nerd, "Baroness Von Sketch Show Season 4 Episode 3," YouTube, February 28, 2020, https://tinyurl.com/4pdtjy6t.

50 ". . . fat mass increases and muscle mass decreases." Marie-Pierre St-Onge and Dympna Gallagher, "Body Composition Changes with Aging: The Cause or the Result of Alterations in Metabolic Rate and Macronutrient Oxidation?," *Nutrition* 26, no. 2 (2010): 152–55, https://doi.org/10.1016/j.nut.2009.07.004.

50 ". . . and even eating behaviors." Hana Ames, "Menopause and Cholesterol: Link, Management, and Prevention," Medical News Today, MediLexicon International, January 14, 2022, https://

tinyurl.com/5n7b8yks; Tara D'Eon and Barry Braun, "The Roles of Estrogen and Progesterone in Regulating Carbohydrate and Fat Utilization at Rest and during Exercise," *Journal of Women's Health & Gender-Based Medicine* 11 (2002): 225–37, https://doi.org/10.1089/152460902753668439.

50 "... roles in keeping us healthy." Stacy Julien, "Your Fat Has Health Benefits," AARP, April 18, 2017, https://tinyurl.com/4z9fjm4d.

50 "... whole-body metabolism in later years." "Slowing or Reversing Muscle Loss," Mayo Clinic, April 10, 2014, https://tinyurl.com/594thd3a.

67 "... fee-for-service, volume-based system." Applewhite, *This Chair Rocks*, 96.

68 "The other 80 percent? Lifestyle." Dan Buettner and Sam Skemp, "Blue Zones: Lessons from the World's Longest Lived," *American Journal of Lifestyle Medicine* 10, no. 5 (July 7, 2016): 318–21, https://doi.org/10.1177/1559827616637066.

69 "... improve cognition, and even lower anxiety." "Benefits of Physical Activity," Centers for Disease Control and Prevention, November 1, 2021, https://tinyurl.com/2w3zcj5k.

69 "... was key to their healthy longevity." Dan Buettner, *The Blue Zones: 9 Lessons for Living Longer from the People Who've Lived the Longest* (Washington, DC: National Geographic, 2012), 266.

72 "... the National Institute of Aging, and the National Science Foundation." "Martin E. P. Seligman," Positive Psychology Center, https://tinyurl.com/2r3y3hyp.

73 "... and finding a new doctor." Applewhite, *This Chair Rocks*, 113.

## Chapter 5

78 "... ideal beauty is ideal because it does not exist." Naomi Wolf, *The Beauty Myth: How Images of Beauty Are Used Against Women* (New York: HarperCollins, 2011), 176.

78 "... suffering from eating disorders are men." Wolf, *The Beauty Myth*, 8.

80 "No wonder other women refuse to tolerate this tyrant." Marianna Cerini, "From Rainbow to Gray: The Evolution of Hair Dye," CNN, March 25, 2020, https://tinyurl.com/ytc3kbpj.

80 "... *think* about this and what it implies." Anne Kreamer, *Going Gray: How to Embrace Your Authentic Self with Grace and Style* (New York: Little, Brown, 2009), 24.

84 "... naturally beautiful white hair and not coloring it." Kreamer, *Going Gray*, 191.

93 "... in order to fit in at the office." Joy Media Collective LLC, The Official CROWN Act, https://www.thecrownact.com/.

93 "... too religious, or not religious enough." Virginia Villa, "Women in Many Countries Face Harassment for Clothing Deemed Too Religious—or Too Secular," Pew Research Center, December 16, 2020, https://tinyurl.com/3tuptj9m.

94 "... let her hair go silver during the pandemic." Robyn Doolittle, "Lisa Laflamme 'Going Grey' Questioned by CTV Executive, Says Senior Company Official," *The Globe and Mail*, 24 August 2022, https://tinyurl.com/mr293ruc.

94 "... reflect her individual biological age." Jeanette Leardi, "From the Catcall to the Catacomb," Jeanette Leardi (website), September 15, 2022, https://tinyurl.com/ydjbew7p.

## Chapter 6

105 "... a docking station for spiritual awareness." Lisa Miller, *The Awakened Brain: The New Science of Spirituality and Our Quest for an Inspired Life* (New York: Random House, 2021), 7.

105 "... that contributes to our mental health." Miller, *The Awakened Brain*, 58.

106 "... the most important implications for aging." Andrew B. Newberg, "Spirituality and the Aging Brain," *Generations: Journal of the American Society on Aging* 35, no. 2 (2011): 83–91, https://www.jstor.org/stable/26555779.

119 "... forced labor in the transatlantic slave trade." "Slave Trade," United Nations, accessed January 19, 2023, https://tinyurl.com/344bave8.

119 "... of the societies of the enslaved." Maureen Warner-Lewis, *Guinea's Other Suns: The African Dynamic in Trinidad Culture* (Kingston, Jamaica: The University of the West Indies Press, 2015).

## Chapter 7

130 "... connect in genuine friendship and love." Vivek H. Murthy, *Together: The Healing Power of Human Connection in a Sometimes Lonely World* (New York: Harper Wave, 2020), 31.

130 ". . . then again when we're old." Kira M. Newman, "How Loneliness Changes across Your Lifetime," Greater Good, August 1,
2018, https://tinyurl.com/b2vxk5jk.

131 ". . . occasional visit provided contentment enough." Newman,
"How Loneliness Changes across Your Lifetime."

131 ". . . have significant impacts on our health, as well." Christina
Ianzito, "Former Surgeon General Vivek Murthy on Loneliness,"
AARP, June 16, 2020, https://tinyurl.com/44md64uh.

131 ". . . and without it there is suffering." Brené Brown, *Daring Greatly:
How the Courage to Be Vulnerable Transforms the Way We Live,
Love, Parent, and Lead* (Sheridan, WY: Gotham Books, 2012), 7.

131 ". . . it requires you to *be* who you are." Brené Brown, *Braving the
Wilderness: The Quest for True Belonging and the Courage to Stand
Alone* (New York: Random House, 2017), 40.

133 ". . . are more likely to have health problems." G. Oscar
Anderson and Colette E. Thayer, "Loneliness and Social
Connections: A National Survey of Adults 45 and Older,"
AARP Research, September 2018, https://doi.org/10.26419/
res.00246.001.

133 ". . . those who feel connected are more optimistic, creative, and
joyful." Murthy, *Together*, xvii.

136 ". . . reminds of us of our value and purpose." Murthy, xii.

140 ". . . have better heart health and reduced stress." Summer Allen,
"Is Gratitude Good for Your Health?," Greater Good, March 5,
2018, https://tinyurl.com/7xcy2574.

## Chapter 8

151 ". . . ('the merchant of death is dead!')." The Editors of Encyclopaedia, "Alfred Nobel," in *Encyclopaedia Britannica*, 23 April 2022,
https://tinyurl.com/f5cem9sn.

151 ". . . developing new ways to 'mutilate and kill.' " Evan Andrews,
"Did a Premature Obituary Inspire the Nobel Prize?," History.
com, December 9, 2016, https://tinyurl.com/348msv63.

152 ". . . formation and spreading of peace congresses." Andrews, "Did
a Premature Obituary Inspire the Nobel Prize?"

152 ". . . better sleep, and healthier behaviors." Amanda MacMillan,
"People Age Better If They Have a Purpose in Life," *Time*, August
16, 2017, https://tinyurl.com/3ndu88py.

152 ". . . overall cognition' as we get older." Nathan A. Lewis, Nicholas
A. Turiano, Brennan R. Payne, and Patrick L. Hill, "Purpose in

Life and Cognitive Functioning in Adulthood," *Aging, Neuropsychology, and Cognition* 24, no. 6 (2017): 662–71, https://doi.org/10.1080/13825585.2016.1251549.

152 ". . . myocardial infarction, and disability." Lewis et al., "Purpose in Life and Cognitive Functioning in Adulthood."

152 ". . . may, in fact, add years to it." Patrick L. Hill and Nicholas A. Turiano, "Purpose in Life as a Predictor of Mortality across Adulthood," *Psychological Science* 25, no. 7 (July 2014): 1482–86, https://doi.org/10.1177/0956797614531799.

156 ". . . that there is meaning in one's life." Viktor E. Frankl, *Man's Search for Meaning* (Boston: Beacon Press, 2006), 103.

156 ". . . the more he actualizes himself." Frankl, *Man's Search for Meaning*, 110.

156 "I will smile at myself." Erin Loechner, "MYkind: A Mission Statement," Design for Mankind, January 2, 2013, https://tinyurl.com/2s34c5jc.

166 ". . . the same way about myself." Tarana Burke, *Unbound: My Story of Liberation and the Birth of the Me Too Movement* (New York: Flatiron Books, 2021), 202–3.

166 ". . . have been introduced in state legislatures." Ellen McCarthy, "#MeToo Raised Awareness About Sexual Misconduct: Has It Curbed Bad Behavior?," *Washington Post*, August 15, 2021, https://tinyurl.com/3s8yjedn.

## Chapter 9

180 ". . . certain types of play over others." Stuart L. Brown and Christopher C. Vaughan, *Play: How It Shapes the Brain, Opens the Imagination, and Invigorates the Soul* (New York: Avery, 2010), 65.

181 ". . . or even pretending and acting." Brown and Vaughan, *Play*, 66–69.

181 ". . . the ones who continue to play." Brown and Vaughan, 71.

183 ". . . new experiences and points of view." Brown and Vaughan, 67.

## Epilogue

201 ". . . strongest predictor of regrets of inaction." Daniel H. Pink, *The Power of Regret* (New York: Riverhead Books, 2022), 154.